UNDERSTANDING EUROPEAN UNION LAW

Fourth Edition

Karen Davies

Routledge
Taylor & Francis Group

Fourth edition published 2011
By Routledge
2 Park Square, Milton Park, Abingdon, Oxon, OX14 4RN

Simultaneously published in the USA and Canada
by Routledge
270 Madison Avenue, New York, NY 10016

Routledge is an imprint of the Taylor & Francis Group, an informa business

Previous editions published by Cavendish Publishing Limited

First edition   2001
Second edition   2003

Previous editions published by Routledge-Cavendish

Third edition   2007

Typeset in Palatino by RefineCatch Limited, Bungay, Suffolk

Printed and bound in Great Britain by TJ International Ltd, Padstow, Cornwall

British Library Cataloguing in Publication Data
A catalogue record for this book is available
from the British Library

Library of Congress Cataloging in Publication Data
A catalog record for this book has been requested

ISBN13: 978–0–415–58245-2 (hbk)
ISBN13: 978–0–415–58234–6 (pbk)
ISBN13: 978–0–203–83641–5 (ebk)

Contents

Table of Cases   *vii*

Table of Legislation   *xvii*

Glossary   *xxi*

Abbreviations   *xxxi*

1   INTRODUCTION   **1**

   I. The significance of EU law   1

   II. The aims of this book   1

   III. How to study EU law   2

   IV. Finding out about EU law   3

   V. Beginning your studies   3

   VI. Conclusions   6

2   THE CREATION OF A EUROPEAN UNION   **7**

   I. Why were the European Communities created?   7

   II. The development of the European Economic Community 10

   III. The EU today   23

3   WHO RUNS THE EU?   **27**

   I. Power sharing   27

   II. The institutional structure of the EU   31

   III. Institutional balance, accountability and democracy
       in the EU   49

   IV. Conclusions   52

4 SOURCES OF UNION LAW   **55**

    I. Primary sources of EU law   56

    II. Secondary sources of EU law   57

    III. Case law of the Court of Justice   64

    IV. General principles of Union law   65

    V. International agreements   68

    VI. Conclusions   68

5 THE RELATIONSHIP BETWEEN UNION LAW AND THE NATIONAL LEGAL SYSTEMS   **71**

    I. The doctrines of direct effect and supremacy   71

    II. Conclusions   84

6 ENFORCING UNION LAW   **87**

    I. Enforcing European law rights before national courts   87

    II. Preliminary references/rulings   91

    III. Enforcement actions against Member States (Arts 258-260 TFEU)   97

    IV. Actions against EU institutions: judicial review of the acts and omissions of Union bodies   101

    V. Conclusions   112

7 FREE MOVEMENT OF GOODS   **115**

    I. The elimination of pecuniary (monetary) barriers to trade   116

    II. The elimination of non-pecuniary barriers to trade   122

    III. Conclusions   137

8 FREE MOVEMENT OF PERSONS   **139**

    I. Gaining the right to 'move freely'   140

    II. Free movement: workers' rights (Arts 45 to 48 TFEU)   143

    III. Free movement: limitations on workers' rights   153

    IV. Enforcing workers' rights to free movement   158

V. Free movement and the rights of 'non-economically
active' citizens   158

VI. Freedom of establishment and the provision of services   162

9   REVISION AND EXAMS   **171**

I. Revision   171

II. Examination technique   172

Index   175

Table of Cases

Adams v Commission (Case 145/83) [1985] ECR 3539;
[1986] 1 CMLR 506 . . . . 110, 112

Adeneler and Others v Ellinikos (Case C-212/04) [2006] IRLR 716 81

Adoui and Cornuaille v Belgian State (French Prostitutes case)
(Cases 115 and 116/81) [1982] ECR 1665; [1982] 3 CMLR 631 155

Alfons Lutticke v Commission (Case 48/65) [1966]
ECR 19 . . . . 97, 107, 109, 111

Alpine Investments (Case C-384/93) [1995] ECR I-4101 168

Amministrazione delle Finanze dello Stato v San Giorgio
(San Giorgio case) (Case 199/82) [1983] ECR 3595; [1985]
2 CMLR 658 . . . . 89, 90, 121

Amministrazione delle Finanze dello Stato v Simmenthal
(Case 106/77) [1978] ECR 629 73

Arblade (Cases C-369 and C-376/96) [1978] ECR 629 168

Arsenal v Reed (No 2) [2003] 91

Barber v Guardian Royal Exchange (Case C-262/88)[1990]
ECR I-1889; [1990] 2 CMLR 513 92

Bauhuis (Case 46/76) [1977] ECR 5 119

Baumbast v Secretary of State for the Home Department
(Case C-413/99) All ER (D) 80 (Sep) 140, 160

Bergaderm v Commission (C-352/98P) [2000] ECR 1-5291 110

Bettray v Staatssecretaris van Justitie (Case 344/87) [1989]
ECR 1621; [1991] 1 CMLR 459 144

Bonsignore v Oberstadtdirektor of the City of Cologne
(Case 67/74) [1975] ECR 297; [1975] 1 CMLR 472 156

Brasserie du Pêcheur SA v Germany; R v Secretary of State
for Transport ex p Factortame Ltd and Others (Pêcheur
and Factortame) (Cases C-46 and C-48/93)
[1996] 1 CMLR 889 . . . . 83, 85, 89, 90, 97, 112

Bresciani (Case 87/75) [1976] ECR 129; [1976] 2 CMLR 62 119

Broekmeulen (Case 246/80) [1981] ECR 2311; [1982] 1 CMLR 91 . . . . . 92, 96

Bulmer v Bollinger [1974] 2 All ER 1226 93

Calpak (Cases 789 and 790/79) [1980] ECR 1949; [1981] 1 CMLR 26 105

Campus Oil Ltd v Minister for Industry and Energy (Case 72/83)
[1984] ECR 2727; [1984] 3 CMLR 544 . . . . 133, 136

Centrafarm v Sterling Drug (Case 15/74) [1974] ECR 1183;
[1974] 2 CMLR 480 . . . . 134, 135

Centrafarm v Winthrop (Case 16/74) [1974] ECR 1183;
[1974] 2 CMLR 480 135

Centros Ltd v Erhvervs-Og Selskab-sstyrelser (Case C-212/97)
[1999] ECR I-1459 164

Centrosteel v Adipol (Case C-456/98) unreported 81

CIA Security International (Case C-194/94) [1996] ECR I-2201 . . . . . 81, 85

CILFIT Srl and Lanificio de Gavardo SpA v Ministry of Health
(Case 283/81) [1982] ECR 3415; [1983] 1 CMLR 472 . . . . 44, 93, 96

Cinéthèque v Federation des Cinemas Francais (Cases 60 and
61/84) [1985] ECR 2605; [1986] 1 CMLR 365. 125

Collins (Case C-138/02) 147, 161

Comet BV v Produktschap voor Siergewassen (Comet)
(Case 45/76) [1976] ECR 2043; [1977] 1 CMLR 533 . . . . 88, 90

Commission v Belgium (Cases 227–30/85) [1988] ECR 1;
[1989] 2 CMLR 797 98

Commission v Belgium (Re Public Employees) (Case 149/79)
[1980] ECR 3881; [1982] ECT 1845 157

Commission v Council, (ERTA case) (Case 22/70) [1971]
ECR 263 . . . . 102, 111

Commission v Council (Case 81/72) [1973] ECR 575 106

Commission v Denmark (Case 302/86) (Danish Bottles case)
[1989] ECR 4607; [1989]1 CMLR 619 125

Commission v France (Case 18/84) [1985] ECR 1339;
[1986] 1 CMLR 605 131

Commission v France (Case 152/78) [1980] ECR 2299;
[1981] 2 CMLR 743 135

Commission v France (Case 167/73) [1974] ECR 359 97

Commission v France (Case C-265/95) (1997) unreported,
9 December 123

Commission v France (French Seamen case) (Case 167/73) 158

Commission v France (French Spirits case) (Case 168/78) 120

Commission v Germany (Animal Inspection Fees case)
(Case 18/87) [1988] ECR 5427 119

Commission v Germany (German Beer case) (Case 178/84)
[1987] ECR 5427 . . . . 133, 136

Commission v Ireland (Buy Irish Campaign) (Case 249/81) . . 115, 123, 124

Commission v Ireland (Irish Souvenirs case) (Case 113/80)
[1981] ECR 1625; [1982] 1 CMLR 706 132

Commission v Italy (1st Art Treasures case) (Case 7/68)
[1968] ECR 423; [1969] CMLR 1 . . . . 116, 134, 136

Commission v Italy (2nd Art Treasures case) (Statistical Levy
case) (Case 24/68) [1969] ECR 193; [1971] CMLR 661 . . . . 118, 119

Commission v Italy (Case 101/84) [1985] ECR 2629;
[1986] 2 CMLR 352 99

Commission v Italy (Case 228/91) [1993] ECR I-2701 133

Commission v Italy (Case C-110/05) 128, 129

Commission v UK, Re UHT Milk (Case124/81) [1983] ECR 203;
[1983] 2 CMLR 1 136

Commission v UK (Case 170/78) [1980] 1 CMLR 716 120

Commission v UK (Case C-246/89R) [1989] ECR 3125;
[1991] 3 CMLR 706 97

Commission v UK (Newcastle Disease case) (Case 40/82)
[1982] ECR 2793; [1982] 3 CMLR 493 . . . . 135, 136

Commission v UK (Tachograph case) (Case 128/78) [1979] ECR 419 98

Conegate Ltd v HM Customs & Excise (Case 121/85)
[1986] ECR 1007; [1986] 1 CMLR 739 . . . . 132, 136

Cordoniu v Council (Case C-309/89) [1994] ECR I-3605 105

Costa v ENEL (Case 6/64) [1964] ECT 585; [1964] CMLR 425 . . . . . 73, 74, 93

Courage Ltd v Crehan (Case C-453-/99) 84, 90

Cowan v Tresor Public (Case 186/87) [1989] ECR 195;
[1990] 2 CMLR 613 167

Cristini v SNCF (Case32/75) ECR 75/01085 153

Da Costa en Schaake NV, Jacob Meijer NV and Hoechst-
Holland NV v Nederlandse Belastingadministratie
(Cases 28–30/62) [1963] ECR 31; [1963] CMLR 224 . . . . . . 64, 91, 94, 96

De Agostini (Cases C-34 to 36/95) 128

Debauve (Case 52/79) [1980] ECR 833 167

Decker (Case C-120/95) [1998] ECR I-1831 125

Defrenne v Sabena (Case 43/75) [1976] ECT 455;
[1976] 2 CMLR 98 .... 76, 77

Deutsche Grammophon v Metro (Case 78/80) [1971] ECR 487 135

Dillenkofer v Germany (Cases T-178, 179 and 188–90/94)
[1996] ECR I-4845; [1996] 3 CMLR 638 84

Doughty v Rolls Royce [1992] 1 CMLR 1045, CA 80

EC v France (Case 90/79) [1981] ECR 283; [1981] CMLR 1 212 120

Echternach and Moritz v Netherlands Ministry for
Education and Science (Case 389 and 390/87) [1989]
ECR 723; [1990] 2 CMLR 305 152

ENU v Commission (Case C-107/91) [1993] ECR I-599 107

Eridania v Commission (Cases 10 and 18/68)[1969] ECR 459 105

European Parliament v Council (Chernobyl case)
(Case C-70/88) [1990] ECR I-2041; [1992] 1 CMLR 91 .... 35, 103

European Parliament v Council (Comitology case)
(Case 302/87) [1988] ECR 5615 35

Factortame see Brasserie du Pêcheur SA v Germany etc; R v
Secretary of State for Transport ex p Factortame Ltd

Familiapress (Case C-368/95) [1997] ECR 1-0000 126

Fink-Frucht v Hauptzollamt München-Landsbergerstrasse
(Case 27/67) [1968] ECR 223 120

Foglia v Novello (Nos 1 and 2) (Cases 104/79 and 244/80)
[1980] ECR 745; [1981] 1 CMLR 45; [1981] ECR 3045;
[1982] 1 CMLR 585 .... 94, 96

Forcheri v Belgium (Case 152/82) [1983] ECR 2323; [1984]
1 CMLR 334 152

Ford Espana v Spain (Case 170/88) [1989] ECR 2305 119

Forster V IB Groep (Case C158/07) (2009) 1 CMLR 32 160

Foster v British Gas (Case C-188/89) [1990] ECR I-3313;
[1990] 2 CMLR 833.. 79, 85

Francovich and Bonifaci v Italy (Cases C-6 and 9/90)
[1991] ECR I-5357; [1993] 2 CMLR 66 ....82, 83, 84, 85, 89,
90, 94, 96, 112

Franz Grad v Finanzamt Traunstein (Case 9/70) [1970] ECR 825. . . . . . 77, 78

Fratelli Constanzo (Case 103/88) [1989] ECR 1839 79

Fratelli Cucchi (Case 77/76) [1977] ECR 987 210 120

Gaal case C-7/94 [1996] ECR I-1031 152

Gebhard v Consiglio (Case C-55/94) [1995] ECR I-4165 . . . . 148, 167

Geddo v Ente Nazionale Risi (Case 2/73) [1973] ECR 865 . . . . 123, 129

Germany v European Parliament & Council (Tobacco
    Advertising cases) (Cases C-233/94 and C-491/01) 30

Germany v Parliament & Council (Tobacco Advertising case)
    (Case C-376/98) [2000] ECRI-8419 60

Gravier v City of Liège (Case 293/83) [1985]ECR 593;
    [1985] 3 CMLR 1; [1985] 1 CMLR 432, Trib of Liège 66

Grimaldi v Fonds des Maladies Professionelles (Case C-322/88)
    [1989] ECR 4407 59

Groener v Minister of Education (Case 379/87) [1989] ECR 3967;
    [1990] 1 CMLR 401 146

Groenveld v Produktschap voor Vee en Vlees (Case 15/79)
    [1979] ECR 3409 130

Grzelczyk (Case C-184/99) [2001] ECR 1-6193 160

Handels-OG Kontorfunktionaernesforbund v Dansk
    Arbeejdsgiverforening (Danfoss case) (Case 109/88)
    [1989] ECR 3199 4

Hoekstra (née Unger) v BBDA (Case 75/63) [1964] ECR 177;
    [1964] CMLR 546 . . . . 97, 143

Humblot v Directeur des Services Fiscaux (Case 112/84)
    [1985] ECR 1367; [1986] 2 CMLR 338 . . . . 121, 122

International Fruit Co v Commission (Cases 41–44/70) [1971]
    ECR 411; [1975] 2 CMLR 515 . . . . 105, 111

Internationale Handelsgesellschaft IHG v Einfuhr-und-
    Vorratsstelle für Getreide and Futtermittel (Case 11/70)
    ECR 1125; [1972] CMLR 255 . . . . 65, 66, 67, 73, 74

Ioannidis CASE (Case C 258/04) [2005] All ER (D) 77 (Sep) 161

Jagerskiold v Gustafsson (Case C-97/98) [1999] ECR I-7319 754 116

Jégo Quéré v Commission (Case T-177/01) [2002] ECR II-2365 105

Johnston v Chief Constable of the RUC (Case 222/84) [1986]
  ECR 165 . . . . 79, 89
Jongeneel Kaas v Netherlands (Case 237/82) [1984] ECR 483 130

Keck and Mithouard (Cases C-267 and 268/91) [1993]
  ECR I-6097 . . . . 43, 64, 126, 128, 129, 130
Kempf v Staatssecretaris van Justitie (Case 139/85)
  [1986] ECR 1741; [1987] 1 CMLR 764 143
Knoors v Secretary of State for Economic Affairs (Case 115/78)
  [1979] ECR 399 165
Kobler v Austria (Case C-224/01) [2001] OJ 212/18 83, ... 94
Kolpinghuis Nijmegen (Case 80/86) [1987] ECR 3639;
  [1989] 2 CMLR 18 80
Konsumentombudsmannen v Gourmet International Products
  (Gourmet Foods case) (Case C-405/98) [2001] ECR I-1795 128
Kupferberg (Case 104/81) 78

Leclerc Siplec (Case C-412/93) 128, 129
Levin v Staatssecretaris (Case 53/81) [1982] ECR 1085 143
Luisi and Carbone v Ministero del Tesoro (Joined Cases 286/82
  and 26/83) [1984] ECR 377; [1985] 3 CMLR 52 167
Lyckeskog (Case 99/00) [2002] ECRI-4839 . . . . 93, 96

Mangold (Case C-144/04) 82
Marleasing v La Comercial Internacional (Case C-106/89)
  [1992] ECR I-4135; [1992] 1 CMLR 305 . . . . 81, 85
Marshall v Southampton and South West Hampshire AHA
  (Marshall (No 1)) (Case 152/84) [1986] ECR 723; [1986]
  1 CMLR 688 . . . . 78, 79, 81, 85
Marshall v Southampton and South West Hampshire
  AHA (Marshall (No 2) (Case C-271/91) [1993]
  ECR I-4367; [1993] 3 CMLR 293 . . . . 89, 90, 97
Martinez Sala (Case C-85/96) 160
Meilicke v ADV/ORGA FA Meyer AG (Case C-83/91) 94, 96
Meroni case (Case 14/60 [1961] ECR 133 110
Metock case (Case C-127/08) 141, 151
Michel S v Fonds National de Reclassement Social des
  Handicapes (Case 76/72) 152

Mickelson v Ross (Case C-142/05) 128, 129

Ministère Public v Even and ONPTS (Case 207/78) [1979]
    ECR 2019 146

Morgan, Iris Butcher (Joined Cases C-11/06 and C-12/06)
    [2007] ECR 1-9161 161

Moritz v Netherlands Ministry for Education and Science
    (Case 390/87) [1989] ECR 723 116 152

Netherlands v Reed (Case 59/85) [1986] ECR 1283; [1987]
    2 CMLR 448 146

Nold v Commission (Case 4/73) [1974] ECR 491; [1974]
    2 CMLR 338 .... 67, 103

Nordsee (Case 102/81) [1982] ECR 1095 .... 92, 96

Officier van Justitie v Sandoz (Case 174/82) 133, 136

O'Flynn v Adjudication Officer (Case C-237/94) [1996] ECR I-2617 147

Pardini v Ministero del Commercio con L'Estero (Case 338/85)
    [1988] ECR 2041 94

Parti Ecologiste 'Les Verts' v European Parliament (Case 294/83)
    [1986] ECR 1339 102

Pfeiffer and Others v Deutsches Rotes Kreuz (Cases C-397–403/01)
    [2004] ECR I-8835 81

Piraiki- Patraiki v Commission (Case 11/82) [1985] ECR 207 104

Plaumann v Commission (Case 25/62) [1963] ECR 95; [1964]
    CMLR 29 .... 104, 105, 111

Procureur du Roi v Dassonville (Case 8/74) [1974] ECR 837;
    [1974] 2 CMLR 436; [1975] FSR 191 .... 124, 125, 126, 129, 130

Pubblico Ministero v Ratti (Case 148/78) [1979] ECR 1629;
    [1980] 1 CMLR 96 78

R v Bouchereau (Case 30/77) [1977] ECR 1999; [1977]
    2 CMLR 800 .... 155, 156

R v Henn and Darby (Case 34/79) [1979] ECR 3795; [1980]
    1 CMLR 246 .... 132, 136

R v HM Treasury ex p British Telecom (Case C-392/93)
    All ER (EC) 411; [1996] IRLR 300 84

R v HM Treasury ex p Daily Mail (Case 81/87) [1988]
    ECR 5483; [1989] 3 CMLR 713 183 164

R v Immigration Appeal Tribunal ex p Antonissen
(Case C-292/89) 144

R v London Borough of Ealing and Secretary of State for
Education and Skills, ex p Bidar (Case C-209/03) 147, 152, 160

R v MAFF ex p Hedley Lomas (Case C-5/94) [1996]
ECR I-2553; [1996] 2 CMLR 391 . . . . 84, 130

R v Secretary of State for Transport ex p Factortame Ltd
(Factortame (No 2)) (Case C-213/89) [1990] ECR 1-2433;
[1990] 3 CMLR 1 . . . . 74, 97, 163

R v Thompson and Others (Case 7/78) [1979] 1 CMLR 47 . . . . 132, 136

Razzouk and Beydouin v Commission (Cases 75a and 117/82)
[1984] ECR 1509 66

Reed case (Case 59/85) [1985] ECR 1283 150

Rewe-Zentral v Bundesmonopolverwaltung fur Branntwein
(Cassis de Dijon case) (Case 120/78) [1979] ECR 649; [1979]
3 CMLR 494 . . . . 125, 126, 127, 129,
130, 131, 133, 136, 148

Rewe-Zentralfinanz v Landschwirtschaftskammer für das
Saarland (Case 33/76) [1976] ECR 1989; [1977] 1 CMLR 533 . . . . 89, 90

Rewe-Zentralfinanz v Landschwirtschaftskammer (San José
Scale) (Case 4/75) [1975] ECR 843; [1977] 1 CMLR 599 . . . . 133, 136

Reyners (Jean) v Belgian State (Case 2/74) [1974] ECR 631;
[1974] 2 CMLR 305 . . . . 76, 85, 166

Rheinmuhlen-Dusseldorf (Cases 146 and 166/73) [1974]
1 CMLR 523 92

Richardt (Case C-367/89) [1991] ECR I-4601 133

Roberts v Tate & Lyle Industries (Tate & Lyle case)
(Case 151/84) [1986] ECR 703; [1986] 1 CMLR 714 79

Roman Angonese v Cassa di Risparmio di Bolzana Spa
(Case C-282/98) unreported 158, 166

Roquette Frères v Council (Case 138/79) [1980] ECR 33333 . . . . 62, 103

Royer (Case 48/75) [1976] ECR 497; [1976] 2 CMLR 619 . . . . 162, 164

Rutili v Ministre de l'Interieur (Case 36/75) [1975]
ECR 1219; [1976] 1 CMLR 140 . . . . 66, 155

Sayag v Leduc (Case 9/69) [1969] ECR 329 109

Schloh (Case 50/85) 124

Schmidberger v Austria (Case C-112/00) [2003] ECR I-5659 125

Schneider v Commission (Case T-351/03) 111

Schoppenstedt v Commission (Case 5/71) [1971] ECR 975 110

Schumacker (Case 279/93) [1995] ECR I-225 148

Simmenthal SpA v Commission (Case 92/78) [1979] ECR 777;
    [1980] 1 CMLR 25 . . . . 93, 108

Société Comateb v Directeur General des Douanes et Droites
    Indirects (Cases C-192–218/95) [1997] ECR I-165; [1997]
    2 CMLR 649 122

Société Roquette Frères v Commission (Case 26/74) [1976]
    ECR 677 111

Sotgui v Deutsche Bundespost (Case 152/73) [1974] ECR 153
    Stanton v INASTI (Case 143/87) [1988] ECR 3877; [1989]
    3 CMLR 761 . . . . 157, 164

Stauder v City of Ulm and International Handelsgesellschaft
    (Case 29/69) [1969] ECR 419; [1970] CMLR 112 66

Steymann v Staatssecretaris van Justitie (Case 196/87) [1988]
    ECR 6159; [1989] 1 CMLR 449 144

Stork v High Authority (Case 1/58) [1965] ECR 405 67

Thieffry v Conseil de L'Ordre des Avocats à la Cour de Paris
    (Case 71/76) [1977] ECR 765; [1977] 2 CMLR 373 164

Toepfer and Getreide-Import Gesellschaft v Commisson
    (Cases 106 & 107/63) [1965] ECR 405 104

Topfer v Commission (Case 112/77) [1978] ECR 1019 65

Torfaen v B&Q (Case 145/88) 126

Trojani v Centre public d'aide sociale (Case C-456/02) [2004]
    ECR I-7573 163

TWD Textilwerke Deggendorf (Case C-188/92) [1994]
    ECR I-833 108

UNECTEF v Heylens (Case 222/86) [1987] ECR 4097; [1989]
    1 CMLR 901 165

Unilever Italia (Case C-443/98) 82, 85

Union de Pequeños Agricultores v Council (UPA case)
    (Case C-50/00P) [2002] ECR I-6677 104

Union Royale Belge des Sociétés de Football Association
    ASBL v Bosman (the Bosman case) (Case C-415/93)
    148, [1995] ECR I-4921; [1996] 1 CMLR 645 . . . . 158, 166

Van Binsbergen v Bestuur van de Bedrijfsvereniging voor de
Metaalnijverheid (Case 33/74) [1974] ECR 1299; [1975]
1 CMLR 298 . . . . 148, 169

Van Duyn (Yvonne) v Home Office (Case 41/74) [1974]
ECR 1337; [1975] 1 CMLR 1 . . . . 76, 78

Van Gend en Loos v Nederlandse Administratie der
Belastingen (Case 26/62) [1963] ECR 1; [1963]
CMLR 105 . . . . .45, 64, 72, 73, 75, 76,
77, 78, 80, 85, 91, 96, 121

Variola Variola SpA v Amministrazione delle Finanze
(Case 34/73) [1973] ECR 981 58

Vlassopoulou (Case 340/89) [1991] ECR 2357 165

Von Colson and Kamann v Land Nordrhein-Westfalen
(Case 14/83) [1984] ECR 1891; [1986] 2 CMLR 430 . . . . 80, 89, 96

Wachauf case (Case 5/88) [1989] ECR 2609 67

Walrave and Koch v Association Union Cycliste Internationale
(Case 36/74) ECR 12405; [1975] 1 CMLR 320 166

Webb, Criminal Proceedings Against (Case 279/80) 148

Wohrmann and Lutticke v Commission (Cases 31 and 33/62) 108

Zhu and Chen v Sec of State for Home Dept (Case C-200/02)
[2004] ECR 1-09925 160

Table of Legislation

Budgetary Treaty 1970 56

Budgetary Treaty 1975 56

Charter of Fundamental
  Rights of the EU 23, 67

Constitution for Europe
  (draft) 18–19

Directive 68/1612 161

Directive 70/50/EEC
  (Restrictions on imports)
  Art 2(1) 124

Directive 77/249/EEC 165

Directive 93/7/EEC 134

Directive 98/5/EC 165

Directive 2004/38 (Citizens'
  Rights of Free
  Movement) 142, 143, 158,
                              161, 166
  Art 2 . . . . 150, 160
  Art 2(b) 147
  Art 3 . . . . 147, 150, 160
  Art 4 . . . . 145, 159
  Art 5 . . . . 145, 151, 159
  Art 6 . . . . 144, 151, 159
  Art 7 . . . . 151, 159, 164
  Art 8 145
  Arts 8–11 159
  Art 10 151
  Art 12 152
  Arts 12–14 159

Art 13 153
Art 14 144
Art 15 159
Art 16 . . . . 149, 151, 159
Art 17 . . . . 149, 151
Art 18 . . . . 151, 153
Art 23 151
Art 24 . . . . 146, 152, 153, 160
Art 24(2) 160
Art 27 154
Art 28 154
Art 29 156
Art 30 155
Art 31 155
Art 32 155
Chapters IV and V 160

Directive 2006/123 . . . . 163, 167

EURATOM Treaty 1957 9, . . . 10, 56

European Coal and Steel
  Community (ECSC)
  Treaty 1951 . . . . 8–9, 10, 56

European Convention on
  Human Rights 7, 66, 67

Laeken Declaration 2001 19

Luxembourg Compromise 39

Merger Treaty 1965 . . . . . 10–11, 56

Regulation 1612/68/EEC
  (Rights of access to and
  conditions of employment) . . . 143

Arts 1 and 2 145
Art 3 146
Arts 7–9 146
Art 12 152

Regulation 3911/92/EEC 134

Schengen Treaty 1985 140

Single European
  Act 1986 . . . . 11–13, 56

Treaty of Amsterdam
  1997 . . . . 15–17, 56

Treaty Establishing the
  European Community,
  Art 234 22

Treaty Establishing the European
  Community (TEC) 15–16, 56
  Art 10 . . . . 90, 96
  Art 12 66
  Art 13 66
  Art 17 141
  Art 30 127
  Art 34(2) 66
  Art 95 60
  Art 141 66
  Art 220 . . . . 44, 65
  Art 226 22
  Art 227 22
  Art 228 22
  Art 230 . . . . 17, 65, 105, 108
  Art 281 68
  Art 288 66
  Art 300 68

Treaty on European
  Union 1992 (TEU)
  (Maastricht Treaty) 4, 13–15,
                              56, 159
  Art 1 20
  Art 2 . . . . 20, 67
  Art 3 20
  Arts 3–6 31

Art 4 . . . . .20, 27, 83, 90,
                              96, 97, 100
Art 5 . . . . .21, 26, 29,
                              30, 31, 151
Art 6 . . . . 21, 23, 67
Arts 9–12 . . . . 23, 51
Art 10 50
Art 12 21
Art 13 . . . . 21, 31, 36
Arts 13–19 21
Art 14 . . . . 32, 48
Art 15 36
Arts 15–16 . . . . 36, 48
Art 16 . . . . 37, 39, 48
Art 17 . . . . 17, 35, 40, 48
Art 19 . . . . 43, 48, 64, 65
Art 45(d) 149
Art 47 . . . . 20, 68
Art 48 22
Art 49 21
Art 50 21
Art 267 22
Art 288 22
Protocol No 2 . . . . 21, 30

Treaty on the Functioning of the
  European Union (TFEU) . . . 17, 56
  340(1) 109
  340(2) 109
  Art 2 . . . . 29, 66
  Arts 2–6 29
  Art 3 . . . . 21, 29
  Arts 3–6 27
  Art 4 . . . . 21, 29
  Art 5 29
  Art 6 . . . . 21, 29
  Arts 7–11 20
  Art 15 23
  Art 17 41
  Art 18 . . . . .66, 145, 147, 152,
                              160, 161, 168
  Art 19 66
  Art 20 . . . . 141, 142, 150, 161

Art 21 . . . . .139, 140, 142, 147, 159, 160
Art 22 62
Art 24 22
Art 26 . . . . 115, 139
Arts 26–37 115
Art 28 116
Arts 28–33 116
Art 29 116
Art 30 . . . . .117–18, 119, 120, 121, 134
Art 31 62
Art 34 . . . . . . .72, 122, 123, 124–9, 130, 132, 133, 134, 136
Arts 34–36 122–3
Art 35 . . . . .122, 123, 129, 130, 132, 136
Art 36 . . . . .122, 128, 130, 132, 134, 135, 136, 155
Art 40 66
Art 45 . . . . .144, 145, 151, 156, 157, 158, 161, 163
Arts 45–48 142
Arts 45–62 139
Art 45(3) 145, 153, 154, 156–7, 166
Art 45(3)(c) 145
Art 45(4) 157, 161
Art 46 . . . . 60, 61
Art 49 . . . . . 77, 162, 163, 164, 166
Arts 49–55 . . . . 142, 162, 169
Arts 49–62 169
Art 51 166
Arts 51–54 168
Art 53 . . . . 165, 166
Art 54 . . . . 163, 164
Art 56 . . . . 167, 168, 169
Arts 56–62 . . . . 142, 162, 166, 169
Art 57 . . . . 167, 169
Art 62 168
Arts 101–102 113
Art 106 62
Art 110 . . . . 120–1, 122

Art 113 60
Art 114 60
Art 157 . . . . 66, 76
Art 177 62
Art 216 68
Arts 223–234 . . . . 32, 48
Arts 223–287 21
Arts 224–250 48
Art 225 33
Art 226 35
Arts 226–228 122
Art 227 . . . . 35, 108
Art 228 35
Art 230 34
Art 231 63
Art 234 35
Arts 235–236 . . . . 36, 48
Arts 237–243 . . . . 37, 48
Art 238 . . . . 39, 64
Arts 244–250 40
Art 249 56
Arts 251–281 . . . . 43, 48
Art 256 45
Art 258 . . . . .22, 42, 97–8, 99, 100, 101
Arts 258–260 . . . . 87, 97, 100, 158
Art 259 . . . . 22, 99, 100
Art 260 . . . . 22, 99, 100
Art 263 . . . . .17, 30, 39, 49, 65, 101, 102, 103, 107–8, 109, 113
Arts 263–266 87
Art 263(4) 102, 105, 112
Art 264 . . . . 102, 106, 111
Art 265 . . . . . 101, 106–8, 111, 112
Art 266 . . . . 106, 107
Art 267 . . . . .22, 75, 79, 87, 91, 92, 96, 108
Art 267(2) 93
Art 267(3) 93
Art 277 111
Art 279 101
Arts 282–287 46

Arts 285–287 46
Art 288 . . . . 22, 55, 57, 58, 59,
73, 77, 78, 102,
104, 105
Art 289 . . . . . 22, 34, 49, 61, 62, 63
Art 291 21
Art 294 . . . . 22, 38, 61, 62, 63
Art 300 47
Arts 300–304 47
Arts 305–307 47
Arts 308–309 47–8
Art 314 34
Art 340 . . . . . 66, 84, 106, 109, 111
Art 345 134
Art 352 60

Protocol No 2 30
Title 1 29
Treaty of Lisbon . . . 4, 19–23, 56, 57
Treaty of Nice 2000 . . . . 17, 56
Treaty of Paris see ECSC
Treaty 1951
Treaty of Rome 1957
(EEC Treaty) 4, 9–10, 56
Art 12 75
Art 30 75
Art 52 77
Art 119 76
Art 189 73

Glossary

Acquis communautaire	The body of objectives, substantive rules, policies, laws, rights, remedies and case law fundamental to the development of the Union legal order.
Advocates General	Assistants to the Court of Justice, having the same status as judges.
Assembly	Original name given to the European Parliament.
Budget	The Union's revenue and expenditure. The Commission is responsible for submitting a draft budget annually to the Council, which shares budgetary authority with the Parliament.
Charges having equivalent effect	Charges having an equivalent effect to customs duties and, as such, prohibited by Union law.
Charter of Fundamental Rights	Charter setting out rights of EU citizens originally drafted in 2009 and given legal effect in December 2009 by the Treaty of Lisbon.
Citizenship	Citizenship of the Union is dependent on holding nationality of one of the Member States (Art 20 TFEU).
Co-decision procedure	The legislative procedure whereby the European Parliament was given the power to adopt acts jointly with the Council. Introduced by the TEU (Art 251 TEC). Now amended and renamed the 'Ordinary' legislative procedure by the Treaty of Lisbon.
Comitology	The process by which the Commission is assisted by committees in the implementation of legislation.
Committee of the Regions	An European Union body whose birth reflects Member States' desire not to respect regional and local identities and prerogatives and also to involve them in the development and implementation of EU policies.

Common Customs Tariff	The common customs duty encircling the EU, charged at the same level no matter where a product is cleared for customs (Art 28 TFEU).
Common policies	Includes policies on agriculture, commerce and transport, established to ensure common principles and aims throughout the Union.
Competition rules	Union rules intended to ensure that competition in the Community is not distorted.
Conciliation Committee	Conciliation Committees may be set up by the Commission under the ordinary legislative procedure with the aim of reaching agreement between the Council and the Parliament in relation to a legislative proposal (Art 294 TFEU).
Consultation procedure	A legislative procedure under which the Council is bound to consult with the European Parliament and take its views into account.
Convergence criteria	Criteria that must be attained by those Member States wishing to join the European Single Currency.
Co-operation procedure	A legislative procedure, introduced by the SEA, giving the Parliament greater influence in the creation of Union legislation. No longer used.
COREPER	Name commonly given to the Committee of Permanent Representatives who carry out tasks on behalf of the Council. They also provide a forum in which legislation can be discussed and agreed.
Council	Often referred to as the Council of Ministers, it has no equivalent anywhere in the world. It is here that the Member States legislate for the Union, set its political objectives, co-ordinate their national policies and resolve differences between themselves and with other institutions.
Court of Auditors	The taxpayers' representative, responsible for checking that the European Union spends its money according to its budgetary rules and regulations and for the purposes for which it is intended.

Council of Europe	A non-EU organisation founded in 1949 and the author of the European Convention on Human Rights. Membership now comprises 47 European countries.
Court of First Instance	Established by the SEA, the Court took over some of the workload of the Court of Justice. Re-named the General Court by the Treaty of Lisbon.
Court of Justice of the EU	Provides the judicial safeguards necessary to ensure that the law is observed in the interpretation and application of the Treaties and, generally, in all of the activities of the Union. (Normally referred to as the 'Court' with a capital C.)
Customs Union	An area where barriers to trade have been eliminated, as exists between the Member States (Arts 28 TFEU).
Decisions	Union legislative acts which are binding upon those to whom they are addressed (Art 288 TFEU).
Deepening	The process of increased integration between the Member States.
Democratic deficit	Criticism levelled at the Union in relation to its perceived remoteness from the ordinary citizen, particularly in relation to the creation of legislation.
Decision making	The processes by which decisions are taken or legislative acts are created within the Union.
Direct applicability	A directly applicable provision of European law is one which takes effect within the Member States without the need for incorporation or implementation by national authorities.
Direct effect	A doctrine established by the Court of Justice providing that Union law may provide rights and obligations to individuals, enforceable in national courts.
Direct elections	Democratic elections held to elect the Members of the European Parliament (MEPs).

Directives	Legislative acts that oblige Member States to implement the aims contained within the directive by a stipulated date (Art 288 TFEU).
Distinctly applicable measure (DAM)	Term used to describe restrictive measures, enacted by Member States, which discriminate between nationally produced goods and those originating in other States.
Dualist State	A State, such as the UK, in which international law and national law are considered distinct and separate from one another.
Economic and Monetary Union	The process whereby the economic and monetary policies of the Member States are harmonised, culminating in the introduction of a single currency.
Economic and Social Committee	In accordance with the Treaties, the Committee advises the Commission, the Council and the European Parliament. The opinions which it delivers (either in response to a referral or on its own initiative) are drawn up by representatives of the various categories of economic and social activity in the European Union.
Effet utile	A principle of law developed by the Court of Justice to ensure effective enforcement of Union rules within the Member States.
Enlargement	See Widening.
Euratom	European Community created in 1957 in order to integrate the nuclear industries of the Member States, promoting safety, research, etc.
European Central Bank	The decision-making body in relation to European Monetary Union, responsible for implementing the monetary policy of the Union.
European Coal and Steel Community	European Community created in 1951 in order to integrate the coal and steel industries of the Member States.
European Commission	A Community institution which has three distinct functions: initiator of proposals for legislation, guardian of the Treaties, and the

	manager and executor of Union policies and of international trade relations.
European Community (EC)	Community created in 1957 by the Treaty of Rome. Once named the European Economic Community (renamed by the TEU) in order to integrate the economies of the Member States. Now part of the European Union (Treaty of Lisbon).
European Communities Act	Enacted in the UK in 1972 in order to incorporate the law of the European Union into the law of the UK.
Euro	European unit of currency.
European Convention on Human Rights	Signed under the aegis of the Council of Europe. While the Union has not yet acceded to the Convention, respect for fundamental human rights has been formalised by the Treaty of Lisbon, which also provides authority for the Union to accede.
European Council	The name given to the meetings of the Heads of State of the Member States. Over the last two decades, its summit meetings have played a crucial role in the development of the EU.
European Investment Bank	The European Union's financing institution; it provides loans for capital investment, promoting the Union's balanced economic development and integration.
European Parliament	The directly elected democratic expression of the political will of the peoples of the European Union; the largest multinational Parliament in the world.
General principles	A body of unwritten principles supplementing Union legislation and developed by the Court of Justice from the threads found in the Treaties, the laws of the Member States and international law.
Harmonisation	The process of approximation laws throughout the Member States in order to ensure the establishment and effective functioning of the internal market.

High Authority	The original name for what has become the European Commission.
Indirect effect	Doctrine developed by the Court of Justice requiring national courts to interpret national legislation in the light of European directives.
Indistinctly applicable measure (IDAM)	Restrictive measures enacted by Member States, which apply equally to domestically produced goods and those produced in other States.
Institutions	Seven institutions that have been afforded powers by the Treaties in order to ensure aims set out in the EU Treaty are realised.
Intergovernmental conference	Conferences of the Heads of State of the Member States held with the specific purpose of amending the primary legislation of the EU.
Intergovernmental organisation	A body which reaches decisions through co-operation and consensus with its membership.
Intergovernmentalism	A theory of integration under which the Member States take decisions by co-operation and consensus.
Internal market	The creation of an internal market is the first of three stages in the creation of a European Union, the others being monetary and political union. It involves uniting the markets of the Member States into a single economic area without internal frontiers.
Judicial review	Term commonly used to describe the various actions available to the Court of Justice in order to review the legality of acts of the institutions.
Locus standi	The right to be heard in court proceedings.
Luxembourg Accords/ Compromise	Agreement reached, in 1966, following the French refusal to accept majority voting in the Council. It allowed Member States to request that decisions be reached by unanimity, rather than majority, when an issue was considered to be of major national interest.
Measures having equivalent effect	Measures having an equivalent effect to quantitative restrictions on trade and held to

	include State measures which discriminate against imports (DAMs) and those which treat imports and domestic goods alike (IDAMs) (Arts 34 & 35 TFEU).
Monist State	A State in which international law is incorporated into the national legal system as soon as it is ratified.
Multi-speed Europe	A term used to describe the system whereby a group of Member States is willing to make an advance in the assumption that other States will follow later. Also known as 'variable geometry'.
Official Journal	A publication of the European Union in which Regulations and Directives must be published, together with other legislative and non-binding acts.
Ombudsman	Every citizen of each Member State is both a national and a European citizen. One of the rights of all European citizens is to apply to the European Ombudsman if they are victims of an act of 'maladministration' by the institutions or bodies.
Preliminary reference	A term describing the procedure by which national courts may request a ruling from the Court of Justice on the interpretation of primary and secondary legislation and on the validity of secondary legislation (Art 267 TFEU).
Purposive method of interpretation	Method of legislative interpretation favoured by the Court of Justice in which the provision of Union law must be put into context and interpreted in the light of the law as a whole. Also alluded to as the teleological or contextual method.
Qualified majority voting	A procedure for reaching agreement in Council by which each Member State's votes are weighted to reflect the population of that State.
Quantitative restriction	Non-pecuniary restrictions placed on goods by virtue of their crossing a frontier, for example, quotas and total bans (Arts 34 & 35 TFEU).

Regulations	Legislative acts of the institutions of the EU which take effect in all Member States without the need for enacting measures on the part of those States (Art 288 TFEU).
Schengen Agreement	An agreement between a number of Member States to abolish checks at common borders in order to achieve free movement of persons.
Single European Act	Amending Treaty signed in 1986 by the Member States. Its main aim was to speed up integration in the (then) Community and it also laid down provisions relating to political co-operation.
Soft law	Rules which have no binding force, but which may nevertheless have practical effects.
Subsidiarity	A principle ensuring that decisions are taken as close as possible to the citizen in areas which are not in the exclusive competence of the Union.
Supranationalism	A theory of integration involving power moving from the Member States to the institutions.
Supremacy	A doctrine developed by the Court of Justice, providing that, where Union law and national law conflict, Union law will take precedence.
Teleological	Derived from the Greek word *telos*, meaning 'end' or 'purpose'.
Transparency	A term used by the institutions to denote openness in their workings. It includes a commitment to access to information.
Treaty of Amsterdam	An amending Treaty introduced in 1999. Its main aims are to place the interests of workers and citizens at the heart of the Union, to remove existing barriers to free movement while improving security, give the Union a greater voice on the world stage and ensure that the institutions are as effective and efficient as possible in preparation for enlargement.
Treaty on European Union	Signed in 1992, the Treaty not only amended TEC, but also created the European Union.

Treaty of Nice	Signed in 2000, came into effect in February 2003, an amending Treaty with the aim of facilitating the enlargement of the EU.
Twin pillars	The 'twin pillars' of direct effect and supremacy of EU law.
Union competence	The Union is based on the principle of limited powers which are specifically attributed to it by the Treaties. Before the Union may take action, it must ensure that it has been provided with the authority to do so (Arts 2–6 TFEU).
Union law	The rules of the EU legal order including primary and secondary legislation, general principles of law and case law of the Court of Justice. Also known as the acquis.
Variable geometry	See Multi-speed Europe.
Widening	A term used to describe the enlargement of the EU.

Abbreviations

AG	Advocate General
Art	Article
CCT	common customs tariff
CFI	Court of First Instance
CHEE	charge having equivalent effect
CMLR	Common Market Law Review
CoA	Court of Auditors
CoR	Committee of Regions
COREPER	Committee of Permanent Representatives
CU	Customs Union
DAM	distinctly applicable measure
DG	directorate-general
EC	European Community/European Council
ECB	European Central Bank
ECHR	European Convention for the Protection of Human Rights and Fundamental Freedoms/European Court of Human Rights
ECJ	European Court of Justice
ECOSOC	Economic and Social Committee
ECR	European Court Reports
ECSC	European Coal and Steel Community
EEC	European Economic Community
EIB	European Investment Bank
EMU	European Monetary Union

EP	European Parliament
ESCB	European System of Central Banks
EU	European Union
EURATOM	European Atomic Energy Community
FR	Fundamental Rights
GP	General Principles of EU law
IDAM	indistinctly applicable measure
IGC	intergovernmental conference
IPR	intellectual property right
MEP	Member of the European Parliament
MHEE	measure having equivalent effect
MS	Member State
NATO	North Atlantic Treaty Organization
OEEC	Organisation for Economic Co-operation
OJ	Official Journal QMV qualified majority voting
QMV	qualified majority voting
QR	Quantitative Restrictions
RGM	relevant geographical market
SEA	Single European Act 1986
TEC	European Community Treaty
TEU	Treaty on European Union 1992 (Maastricht Treaty)
TFEU	Treaty on the Functioning of the European Union
ToA	Treaty of Amsterdam 1997
ToN	Treaty of Nice 2000

1 Introduction

I. THE SIGNIFICANCE OF EU LAW

The UK's membership of the European Union (EU) means that European Union law has become an integral source of UK national law. Knowledge and understanding of the law of the Union is therefore indispensable to all lawyers in the United Kingdom.

II. THE AIMS OF THIS BOOK

In recognition of the importance of EU law, it is vital that law students have a solid grounding in its principles. Many students appear to find the study of Union law rather alarming, however, which is perhaps understandable given the differences of approach and language that exist between the Union's legal system and that of the United Kingdom.

Students of EU law should, however, take heart. The Union goes back little more than 50 years and has generally developed with a set of specific aims in mind, which means that it is possible to approach it in a logical, incremental manner. That is not to say that the scope of EU law is narrow. Indeed, it is not and it would be impossible to cover all that it encompasses in any degree of depth in a single volume.

In recognition of the breadth of EU law, the content of most EU law courses is necessarily limited to the principal constitutional and institutional areas of the Union's legal order, together with selected areas of substantive law.

Despite this approach, there are still huge areas of law to cover, and although there are a number of excellent textbooks providing detailed accounts of the law, such texts can be intimidating or overpowering and, consequently, rather daunting to the new student.

While this book aims to provide an account of the same constitutional and institutional principles together with important areas of substantive law, albeit in a less circuitous manner than many texts, a different approach has been taken. At the beginning of each topic, before the legal principles are examined, each area of law is put into context, thus allowing an understanding of relevant issues to be developed.

In addition, at the end of most sections, knowledge and understanding are consolidated by the provision of diagrams or flowcharts, highlighting the main points at issue, and/or 'thinking points' to encourage you to further develop your understanding.

This approach is intended to encourage an understanding of EU law as a whole, allowing students to develop a 'feel' for the subject and, ultimately, resulting in far less rote learning being necessary just before examinations!

III. HOW TO STUDY EU LAW

Your approach to studying EU law can make all the difference to your enjoyment of the course and also to the end result. The subject of the UK's membership of the EU is one of keen debate in the media and it is almost impossible not to have formed some sort of opinion as to whether the UK should be 'in' or 'out'! Certain UK newspapers appear to thrive on discussion as to whether the EU should dictate the shape of the bananas we eat or whether hedgehog-flavoured crisps should be banned and it is often difficult to arrive at the study of European law with an open mind. However, this is an essential prerequisite to successful study!

During your course you will be expected to attend lectures and tutorials. Do not underestimate the importance of these as learning tools. We all learn in various ways, not only through what we read, but also by listening, seeing and doing. Reading various texts, periodicals and so on is essential *but* attending lectures can focus the mind, provide an introduction to a topic, shed light on areas of confusion and afford an alternative point of view!

Similarly, tutorial/seminar attendance has numerous advantages (and attendance is likely to be mandatory, if you wish to stay on the course!). It allows various topics or points to be focused upon, it provides opportunity for discussion, it allows for clarification and is also likely to provide invaluable practice in answering exam-type questions, both essay and problem solving. Be sure not to miss out on these opportunities and don't think that you can 'get away with it' by not spending adequate time preparing for tutorials, as the loss will be yours alone!

IV. FINDING OUT ABOUT EU LAW

1. Resources

There is a wealth of sources of information on EU law. Those enrolled on a structured course will normally be provided with at least an outline list of appropriate textbooks and relevant legal journals.

Make sure you have an up-to-date copy of EU legislation at the *start* of your course. If used regularly, you will find it invaluable. The Treaty on the Functioning of the European Union (TFEU), Treaty on European Union (TEU) and secondary legislation are, in the main, very readable and **you should *always* read the various Treaty articles and secondary legislation as you study them**. The value of reading primary source materials is often underestimated by students who are new to law, so don't lose out by ignoring them.

In addition to more traditional sources of legal information, Internet access has opened up a huge source of materials. The number of websites containing information on Union law appears to grow daily and it is a virtually impossible task to provide a comprehensive list. Do, however, take care only to consult those sites which are *recognised legal databases*. The EU also has its own website, which is a good place to begin, as it also provides a number of links to other relevant sites. The address of this site is http://europa.eu.int. Learning to negotiate the site may take a little time but the benefits can be enormous.

Furthermore, the Union Institutions produce a wealth of literature (including CD-ROMs) on various aspects of the EU, much of which is free. A list of such publications, together with details of how to order, can be found on the Europa website.

V. BEGINNING YOUR STUDIES

1. Coping with jargon

Law students often remark that, when they embark on a course of study of a particular branch of law, not only do they have to take on board new legal principles, statutes, case law and so on, but they also have to cope with legal jargon that is particular to that area of law. This is certainly true of EU law, and students new to the subject may find themselves confused by terminology.

In order to overcome this problem (which can have serious consequences, as students who fail to break through the jargon may never fully understand the law beyond), this book provides a glossary of commonly used terms. *It is advisable to consult this at the beginning of your studies and also to refer to it throughout.*

2. EEC, EC or EU?

One important issue of terminology that needs to be understood from the outset is the difference in name that has been afforded to 'Europe' over the years, that is EEC, EC and EU. The European Economic Community (EEC) was created by the Treaty of Rome in 1957. This Community was subject to a change of name in 1993, following the enactment of the Treaty on European Union, 1992 (TEU, also commonly referred to as the Maastricht Treaty), when it became the European Community (EC). Confusingly, the TEU also created the European Union (EU). Further confusion arises because the EU was, at that time, a complex structure made up of a number of parts, *one* of which was the EC. The EC was therefore part of the EU, but not the same as it! However, since the introduction of the Treaty of Lisbon in December 2009, the EC no longer exists as an entity and has been 'superseded' by the EU. Consequently, **all contemporary references should now be to the EU**. This should become clearer once Chapter 2 has been read and digested!

3. Dealing with case names

In addition to the often oblique terminology which has been adopted by the EU, students of EU law often find the names of the decisions of the Court of Justice of the European Union to be a nightmare!

When it is considered that the EU is comprised of 27 states, and has almost as many official languages, it is understandable that case names should occasionally prove difficult to pronounce and spell. Few lawyers would pretend that Case 109/88, *Handels-OG Kontorfunktionaernesforbund v Dansk Arbeejdsgiverforening*, flows easily off either the tongue or the pen. Despair may be avoided, however, once you understand that many EU law cases have nicknames that are often acceptable for use in examinations (but do check with your tutor). For example, the commonly used and accepted nickname for the above case is *Danfoss* which, I am sure you will agree, is quite manageable!

3. Make sure you know 'where you are going'

Life can be made far easier if we know in which direction we're going. If we are unsure, then life can be very confusing. The same can be said of studying European law. It is not sufficient to know that you are going to study EU

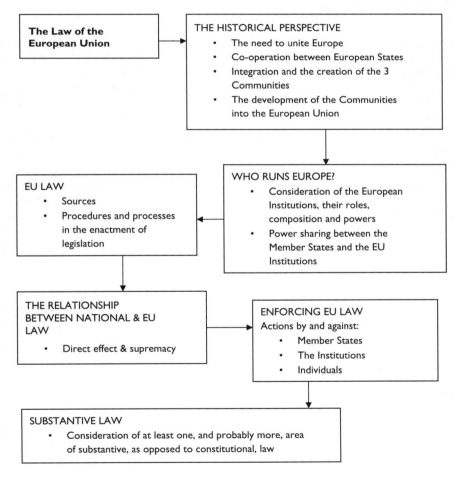

Outline of Typical EU Law Syllabus

law. In order to make studying as painless as possible, and even enjoyable (yes!), you need to have some knowledge of precisely what areas of law you are going to study, *why* you are studying them and also in what order various topics are going to be considered.

If you are provided with a course guide, such information is often contained within it. Generally, undergraduate EU law courses follow a scheme which is roughly that of this book.

VI. CONCLUSIONS

Hopefully, this book will not be seen as just another simplified or insubstantial text but rather as an introduction to European law, which ensures that all who access it provide themselves with firm foundations on which to build greater and deeper knowledge. No strong, high or long-lasting wall was ever built without a sound foundation being put in place first!

Remember that this book does not profess to contain all you will need to know about the law of the European Union but, hopefully, it will provide the desire and the tools to study further. Finally, if there is something you do not understand, please do not let it blight your studies – if you do not know, find a man (or woman) who does, and ASK! Most tutors worth their salt will be only too pleased to help.

2 The Creation of a European Union

I. WHY WERE THE EUROPEAN COMMUNITIES CREATED?

The best way to understand European Union law is to start at the beginning, which inevitably involves consideration of why it exists at all. The idea of a united Europe is certainly not a new one and a variety of leaders have, over the centuries, attempted to achieve European integration. In more modern times, it is possible to highlight the end of the Second World War in 1945 as the catalyst which set in motion events that have led to the creation of a European Union.

The economies of the European States had been devastated by successive wars and the peoples of Europe were anxious to build a peaceful and more stable future for themselves. The United States of America saw a union between various European countries as a means of countering a perceived communist threat from the eastern bloc and, consequently, provided financial aid under what became known as the Marshall Plan. In order to administer this programme of aid the Organisation for Economic Co-operation was set up in 1948, inevitably involving co-operation between recipient States. Other organisations such as the North Atlantic Treaty Organization (NATO), whose aims primarily related to defence, were also created and can be seen as early forms of modern co-operation in Europe.

1. The Council of Europe

Further co-operation between European governments led, in 1947, to the creation of the Council of Europe, an intergovernmental organisation (use the Glossary!) which adopted the European Convention on Human Rights and established the European Court of Human Rights. *It needs to be emphasised from the outset that this organisation is TOTALLY SEPARATE from that which has become known as the European Union*. While undoubtedly performing a valuable role, particularly in the area of human rights, the Council of Europe fell short of what many felt was needed in order to stabilise inter-State relationships and ensure economic regeneration.

2. The First European Community: The European Coal and Steel Community (ECSC)

A plan based on economic co-operation in Europe was proposed by Jean Monnet and taken up by Robert Schuman, the then French Foreign Minister. This embryonic scheme took a functionalist approach (that is integration sector by sector) and involved the integration of the French and German coal and steel industries, as a means of stabilising the relationship between the two countries. The plan allowed the two industries to be closely monitored, ensuring that the capacity of the States to secretly re-arm was reduced. However, as the idea also included ensuring security on a wider European basis, an invitation to participate was proffered to other European countries and the ECSC was finally created by the signing of the Treaty of Paris in 1951. This new Community had an initial membership of six, namely France, Germany, Italy, Belgium, Luxembourg and the Netherlands. (It is interesting to note that the then British Prime Minister, Sir Anthony Eden, had declared that the UK had no need to join, as it was well able to 'stand on its own two feet' – a reference to the UK's links with both its Commonwealth and the USA.)

The creation of the ECSC was particularly significant as it moved away from the more traditional intergovernmental system of co-operation between participating States. Four independent Institutions were created to run the ECSC and the power to control the coal and steel industries was moved from the participating States to those Institutions that comprised a High Authority, an Assembly, a Council and a Court of Justice. The new Community consequently had a supranational, rather than intergovernmental, flavour. (Glossary!) It is interesting to note that, although more than 50 years have gone by since this original transfer of 'sovereign powers' from the States to the Community, as we shall see later, the extent of this transfer of authority still remains a matter of debate and contention within the EU.

While the immediate focus of the ECSC was undoubtedly economic, that is, the creation of a common market in coal and steel, with common policies and the removal of all barriers to trade in those commodities, it should not be forgotten that the contracting States saw economic co-operation as a means to an end. Ensuring that the longer term aims of peace and European unity were achieved was the focus, if not the immediate emphasis, of the Community. This can be evidenced by reference to the Preamble to the Treaty of Paris, which provides that the establishment of an economic community is a 'basis for a broader and deeper community among peoples long divided by bloody conflicts; and to lay the foundations for Institutions which will give direction to a destiny henceforward shared'.

It should be noted that the Treaty of Paris expired in July 2002 and ECSC funds have since been transferred to the EU, to be used for research in sectors relating to the coal and steel industries.

3. Failed moves towards European Defence and Political Communities

Following the creation of the ECSC, further attempts at integration between the contracting States were made, with plans being drawn up for a European Defence Community and European Political Community, involving the creation of a European army and a common European foreign policy. Agreement could not, however, be reached on these matters, and it was not until 1956 that a way forward towards further integration was found. A report was published by an intergovernmental committee chaired by Paul-Henri Spaak, the then Belgian Foreign Minister, detailing plans for a further two communities, the European Atomic Energy Community (EURATOM) and the European Economic Community (EEC).

4. The European Atomic Energy Community (EURATOM)

The EURATOM Treaty was signed in Rome in 1957 by the same six countries that had previously joined together to form the ECSC. The object of this new Community can be summarised as the furtherance of atomic energy for peaceful purposes, together with a commitment to uniform safety standards. Once more, as for the ECSC, the control of each Member State's atomic power industries was passed to four autonomous Institutions, with the Assembly and the European Court of Justice being common to both Communities.

5. The European Economic Community (EEC)

Like EURATOM, the EEC was born as a result of the Spaak Report, and the Treaty establishing the EEC – the EEC Treaty – was signed in Rome (hence often being referred to as the Treaty of Rome) by the same six Member States, on the same day as the EURATOM Treaty. A further similarity lies in the fact that the new Community was to be administered by four independent Institutions upon which the Member States had delegated the right of independent action in certain specified areas. (Once more, the Court and the Assembly were shared between the Communities.)

There was, however, a significant difference between the first two Communities and the EEC. Both the ECSC and EURATOM were limited in their scope, being functionalist in that they had as their aims the creation of a common market in coal and steel and in atomic energy, respectively. The EEC was significantly broader in its approach, in that it was created with the task of working towards integration of *all* aspects of the economies of its Member States, rather than integration of specific industries.

While the vehicle for integration was once more economic, the Preamble to the EEC Treaty continued to make it clear that longer term goals were wider, including a determination to 'lay the foundations of an ever closer union among the peoples of Europe'. This was very much in line with Monnet and Schuman's view that integration of the Member States' economies would spill over into other areas, namely political and social.

II. THE DEVELOPMENT OF THE EUROPEAN ECONOMIC COMMUNITY (EEC)

The term 'European Communities' is used to denote all three Communities, that is, the ECSC, EURATOM and the EEC. This should not be confused with the European Community (EC), which was the name eventually given to the EEC by the later Treaty on European Union (TEU). The Communities have not stood still since their inception and, in order to fully understand the present position, the major milestones in their development need to be considered.

1. The Merger Treaty 1965

The Merger Treaty, which came into effect in 1967, was the first amendment to the Treaties of Paris and Rome. Its main purpose was to merge the Institutions of all three Communities, creating a common Council of

Ministers and a common Commission (formerly known as the High Authority). The remaining two Institutions, the European Parliament (EP, formerly the Assembly) and the Court of Justice (often referred to as the ECJ), already served all three Communities.

2. The Single European Act 1986

The Single European Act (SEA), which came into effect in 1987, was the first substantial revision of the original EEC Treaty. While considerable early success had been enjoyed, progress with regards to further integration had slowed to near-stagnation. This virtual standstill was blamed on a number of factors, both external and internal, including world recession and difficulties relating to decision taking within the EEC, and the SEA can be viewed as a response to such problems.

The SEA contains a number of important provisions, both amending the original Treaties and also laying down provisions for political co-operation between the Member States.

First, the new Treaty formalised European political co-operation by recognising the European Council and providing for twice-yearly meetings. (A note of warning: take care not to confuse the European Council with the 'Council'. The European Council is a separate organisation created in 1974, with a membership composed largely of the Heads of State or Government of the Member States, while the Council is composed of representatives of each Member State at ministerial level.)

The SEA amendments also attempted to ensure increased efficiency and democracy within the institutional framework. A Court of First Instance (CFI) was created to assist the overworked European Court of Justice (ECJ). In addition, a new legislative procedure, known as 'co-operation', was introduced which provided the European Parliament (EP) with increased influence in the legislative process. The EP was also given the right of veto over the accession of new Member States. (Changes to the EP's functions were a response to calls for an enhanced role following the introduction of direct elections for Members of the European Parliament MEPs by citizens of the Member States. The first elections took place in 1979 and were significant in that the EP became the first – and only – Union Institution to receive a direct, democratic mandate.)

In an attempt to revitalise progress towards economic integration, the SEA also introduced an 'Internal Market' to be attained by a set date: 31 December 1992. Also known as the 'Single Market', the Internal Market was intended to take the EEC beyond being merely a customs union (i.e. an area without internal barriers to trade) to a community with complete totality of economic activity. (You may find the terminology here a little confusing: the Common, Single and Internal Market are all terms which have been used to describe Europe's trading area. Thankfully, under the changes introduced by the latest treaty, the Treaty of Lisbon in December 2009, all references should now be to the Internal Market.) The Commission was given a central role in the completion of the Internal Market, thereby increasing its influence in Europe.

It was realised that the creation of a single market would require substantial legislative activity by the Institutions and, with this in mind, the SEA introduced a change to voting procedures in the Council. The use of qualified majority voting (whereby each Council Minister's vote is 'weighted', reflecting the population of the Member State which they represent) was significantly increased and, with the corresponding move away from the need for unanimity, the legislative process was effectively speeded up. (It is far easier and quicker to ensure majority agreement to a legislative proposal than to achieve unanimity.)

The SEA also extended the existing substantive areas of Community competence, formally recognising co-operation in economic and monetary union, social policy, economic and social cohesion (i.e. reducing disparity between the various regions within the Community), research and technological development and action on protection of the environment.

Finally, the Treaty referred to political co-operation, albeit outside formal Community structures. It provided for the inclusion of the

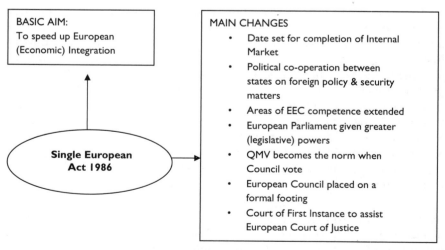

The Single European Act

Commission and EP within the process and also for the development of co-operation in foreign policy and security fields (thus creating the forerunner of the 'three-pillared' EU, which is discussed below).

While the SEA was not without its critics, who decried it as vague and ambiguous, it undoubtedly gave renewed momentum to plans for the economic integration of Europe and also laid important foundations for social and political integration. Institutional changes introduced by the Act supported the supranational nature of the Communities by increasing the influence of both the EP and the Commission while, at the same time, qualified majority voting (QMV) became the 'norm' in Council decision making, decreasing the influence of individual Member States.

3. The Treaty on European Union 1992 (The Maastricht Treaty)

The Treaty on European Union (TEU), also commonly known as the **Maastricht Treaty** after the Netherlands town where it was signed, was created with two broad aims in mind: first, to sustain the momentum created by the SEA and, second, the creation of a new organisation, albeit founded on the original Communities, to be known as the European Union (EU). The Treaty, which took effect in 1993, can be divided into two distinct areas: firstly, that which amended the original EEC Treaty and secondly, that which created a new body – the EU.

i. Changes to the original EEC Treaty

Significantly, the TEU renamed both the European Economic Community (EEC) and the EEC Treaty, removing the word 'Economic' from both. (The EC Treaty is formally known as the **Treaty Establishing the European Community** or **TEC**.) It can be argued that the removal of this term was intended to indicate that, with the process of economic integration nearing completion, the European Community (EC) could now begin to concentrate on further integration in social and political areas.

The TEU also broadened the aims of the Community to include such objectives as environmental protection. In addition, the TEU provided for institutional and legislative changes, together with a timetable for the introduction of European Monetary Union (EMU). New areas of Community competence were introduced, while others were expanded. While the main changes are highlighted below, they will be further discussed, as appropriate, in later chapters.

The EP's involvement in the legislative process was once more increased by extended use of the co-operation procedure (introduced by the SEA) and the introduction of a new procedure known as co-decision, which effectively allowed the EP to 'veto' legislative proposals. In addition, the Parliament was given a right of initiative with regard to legislation, once a monopoly enjoyed by the Commission. The EP was also afforded the power to appoint a European Ombudsman to investigate complaints relating to alleged maladministration on the part of the Community Institutions and their staff. Other changes involving the Institutions included formally recognising the Court of Auditors (CoA) as a Community Institution and the creation of a European Central Bank (ECB). (Further consideration of Union bodies is provided in Chapter 3.)

As part of an attempt to bring the Community closer to the peoples of Europe, the TEU introduced the concept of European citizenship, which is provided to all nationals of the Member States. With regard to issues relating to economic and monetary policy, the path towards EMU was further elaborated and a timetable set for its various stages, climaxing with the adoption of a single currency.

ii. Creation of the European Union

The TEU created a 'three-pillared' structure, originally comprising the following:

Pillar I, made up of the ECSC, EURATOM and the European Community (i.e. the European Communities);

Pillar II, which provided for the development of policies relating largely to the Member States and their relationship with the rest of the world;

Pillar III, which provided for inter-State co-operation on policies including asylum, external border controls, immigration and international fraud together with judicial co-operation on civil and criminal matters, and police co-operation relating to terrorism and drugs.

(*Note that the specific content of these pillars was later subject to further change and has now been dismantled, as discussed in further detail below.*)

In contrast to the EC, the original EU did not have separate legal personality and, with regard to Pillars II and III, there was no transfer of sovereign powers from the Member States to the Institutions. Instead, progress under Pillars II and III relied largely on intergovernmental co-operation and consensus amongst the Member States.

As with the SEA before it, the TEU has been the subject of considerable academic analysis and criticism, not all of it complimentary. Commentators claimed, for example, that the structure of the Union was too complex and

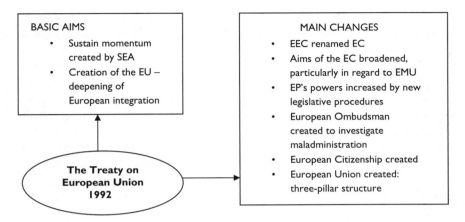

**The Treaty on European Union
(The Maastricht Treaty)**

fragmented and that the 'opt-outs' reduced unity (e.g. the UK's reluctance to join the single currency). On the other hand, the Treaty was praised for measures such as increasing the role of the Parliament, widening the areas of European competence and increased flexibility.

4. The Treaty of Amsterdam 1997

The Treaty of Amsterdam (ToA), which came into effect in May 1999, has been described as a consolidating treaty, its main purposes being to improve processes, increase effectiveness and bring the EU closer to the ordinary person by making it more comprehensible.

Its provisions included a commitment to greater openness in the decision-making processes of the EU (transparency) and the recognition that the Union is based on respect for fundamental rights, democracy and the rule of law. Indeed, membership of the Union was made contingent upon respect for such principles, and the Treaty also declared that the Union must respect human rights protected under the European Convention on Human Rights (ECHR). Any Member State found to be in 'serious and persistent' breach of such rights could now find its own rights, particularly those in regard to voting, suspended. (*Protection of Fundamental Rights has now become an important area for the Union and will be discussed in further detail in Chapter 3.*)

The EC Treaty (TEC) was 'tidied up', with all obsolete provisions being removed. This resulted in an almost complete renumbering of the Treaty and students need to ensure that they know whether Treaty Articles referred to in older journals and books relate to the old or new system of numbering. (It is important to note that publications prior to May 1999 are likely to refer to the 'old' numbering of TEC. Also be aware that the Treaty of Lisbon has resulted in re-numbering of provisions within both the TEU and TFEU.)

Specific changes to the TEC included a new non-discrimination provision that provided the EC with the authority to create secondary legislation aimed at combating discrimination based on sex, racial or ethnic origin, religion or belief, disability, age and/or sexual orientation. Member States were also encouraged to work together to combat unemployment, while issues such as public health and consumer protection were amended.

With regard to the Institutions, the EP was allowed yet further involvement in the legislative process as the use of the co-decision procedure, included by virtue of the TEU, was expanded and simplified.

In an attempt to stem some of the criticisms levelled at the original Pillar structure, a number of changes were made. These largely related to procedures, financing, institutional involvement and international identity, together with a revision of the defence provisions. With regard to Pillar III, a substantial part of the subject matter of the Pillar was incorporated into Pillar I, where it was included in TEC. Pillar III was also renamed Police and Judicial Co-operation in Criminal Matters with areas targeted for 'common action' including terrorism, drugs and arms trafficking, trafficking

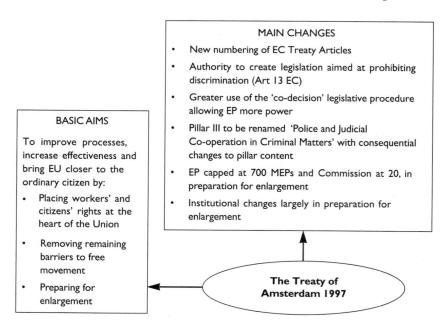

The Treaty of Amsterdam

in persons, offences against children, corruption, fraud and the prevention and combating of racism and xenophobia.

5. The Treaty of Nice 2000

The Treaty of Nice (ToN), which came into effect in February 2003, was enacted with the aim of facilitating, largely through institutional reform, the further enlargement of the EU.

The changes introduced by Nice were described as 'modest' and even 'disappointing' and can be summarised as follows:

- *The decision-making process:* An extension of qualified majority voting in Council, together with a change of procedure, in that any decision needed to receive a specified number of votes (the 'threshold') *together with* the approval of a majority of Member States; a re-weighting of the votes in favour of the larger EU countries; increased use of the co-decision procedure, allowing the EP additional legislative authority.

- *The legal system.* In order to limit delays in obtaining judgments of the Court of Justice, a redistribution of responsibilities between the courts was provided for, allowing the Court of First Instance (CFI, now known as the General Court) to provide preliminary rulings (discussed in Chapter 6) on specific matters.

- *Other institutional changes.* Limits were placed on the size of the Commission and EP. The EP was also placed on an equal footing with the Council and Commission in regard to judicial proceedings under Art 230 TEC (now Art 263 TFEU, discussed further in Chapter 6).

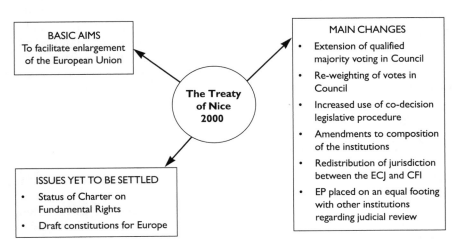

The Treaty of Nice

6. Enlargement

i. UK's application for membership

By the early 1960s, the Member States of the Communities were beginning to enjoy the benefits of membership. A number of non-member European States, including the UK, were becoming aware of the benefits of membership and, in 1961, Britain made its first application to join. General De Gaulle, then President of France, made no secret of his hostility towards British membership, suggesting instead that the UK should continue its association with the Commonwealth and the USA. The UK's application to join was consequently rejected.

A second UK bid to join in 1967 also failed and it was not until January 1973, following De Gaulle's resignation, that the UK (together with Ireland and Denmark) was finally admitted.

ii. Further enlargement

In 1981, Greece joined the EEC, with Portugal and Spain raising the number of Member States to 12 by 1986. Austria, Sweden and Finland joined in January 1995, bringing the total to 15 Member States.

In May 2004, a further 10 States joined the Union, namely the former eastern bloc countries of Estonia, the Czech Republic, Latvia, Lithuania, Hungary, Poland, Slovenia and Slovakia, together with Cyprus and Malta. This prompted Commissioner Gunter Verheugen to conclude that enlargement of the EU was a 'further step towards the fulfilment of an ideal that will bring peace, stability and democracy to the whole area ranging from the Baltic Sea to the Black Sea', demonstrating that the original goals for Europe are as relevant today as they were over half a century ago. In 2007 further enlargement occurred when Bulgaria and Romania joined. At present, applications for membership have been received from a number of other States, including Turkey, Croatia and Macedonia.

7. A Draft Constitution for Europe

Debate on creating a constitution for Europe is not a new issue and the prospect has been considered at various times since the mid-1970s, with the most recent discussions culminating in the Heads of State or Government of the Member States agreeing the text of a '**Treaty Establishing a Constitution for Europe**' in 2004.

In 2001, the Heads of State met at Laeken, Belgium for an IGC. *(Remember to look up any unfamiliar abbreviations or terms in the list of abbreviations/ glossary at the beginning of this book!)* In what become known as the Laeken Declaration, the challenges facing the EU were set out. It was recognised, in particular, that the Institutions needed to bring themselves closer to the peoples of Europe by increasing democracy, transparency and efficiency, while the EU's role on the global stage was also in need of clarification.

The European Council, through the Laeken Declaration, set up a 'European Convention' to consider such challenges, including the status of the EU's Charter of Fundamental Rights, and also to draft a 'Constitution for Europe'. The Convention was a move away from the norm – that is, discussion behind closed doors – to a far more public debate. Indeed, debate was opened to the public, while all official documents where also made public. In addition, the Convention set up numerous working groups and consulted with interested parties such as trade unions, employers' organisations and academics.

In 2003, after 16 months of intensive work, the European Convention produced a draft treaty establishing a 'Constitution for Europe'. This draft treaty was submitted to an IGC and, in October 2004, was unanimously agreed and signed by all Member States and candidate countries.

However, before the Treaty Establishing a Constitution for Europe could enter into force, it had to be ratified by all Member States. In 2005, the peoples of France and the Netherlands rejected the text of the Constitution. In the light of this, the European Council put ratification of the Constitutional Treaty on hold in order for a 'period of reflection' to take place. At a summit held in the summer of 2007, the proposed treaty was formally abandoned *but* it was also decided that moves towards reform would continue.

8. The Treaty of Lisbon

As a result of Europe's continuing commitment to reform, in December 2007 a **'Reform Treaty'** was agreed by all 27 Member States in Lisbon, Portugal. As a consequence of *where* it was agreed, the Treaty has since become known as the Treaty of Lisbon. The Treaty suffered an initial setback in June 2008, when it was rejected by the Republic of Ireland, but, following a second, successful Irish referendum in October 2009, the Lisbon Treaty finally took effect in December 2009. The Treaty introduced a number of changes and an outline of these changes, in areas covered by this book, is provided below.

Area of change/ Development	Overview of Change	Additional Notes
Why was a new treaty needed?	Reform needed to address the 'challenges of the 21st Century'. In particular, to create a more democratic, transparent & efficient Europe, based on rights, values, freedom, solidarity and security, reflecting its place on the global stage	Enacted as a result of the failure of the 'Constitutional Treaty'. To find out more, it is suggested you visit: http://europa.eu/lisbon_treaty/glance/index_en.htm
Change of name	EC Treaty (TEC) was renamed **Treaty on the Functioning of the European Union** (TFEU). The Maastricht Treaty was also amended but its formal name (TEU) remained unchanged	(I) The ToL is *not* a 'stand-alone' treaty: it functioned by **amending** the TEC and the TEU (II) All References to 'Community' amended to 'Union' (**Art 1 TEU**)
Legal personality	**Art 47 TEU** provided the EU with legal personality	Previously, while EC had legal personality, the EU did not
Re-numbering of Treaty Articles	ToL resulted in the re-numbering of both the TEC (now TFEU) & the Maastricht Treaty (TEU)	Refer to a 'table of equivalence' when reading older texts. [Consider whether pre-1999 (as ToA also resulted in re-numbering) or pre-2010]
Structure of EU	'Three-pillar' structure of EU was merged into a single framework (European Union) (**Art 1 TEU**)	'Special Procedures' were maintained in some areas of Pillars II III (Common Foreign and Security Policy; a High Representative to represent the EU in external matters)
Union objectives & values	Refined and set out in **Art 3 TEU. Art 2 TEU** set out the values on which the EU is founded	Respect for human dignity and equality were emphasised
Provisions having 'General Application'	A number of provisions in the TFEU recognised as applying to all within the EU, at all times (**Arts 7 to 17 TFEU**)	These provisions are likely to influence the Court of Justice in interpreting and applying EU law
Duty of the MS	**Art 4 TEU** in effect replaced Art 10 TEC, providing MS with their obligation to	

	comply with EU law, co-operate and do everything in their power to ensure the Union's objectives are attained. **Art 291 TFEU** also provided that the MS 'shall adopt all measures necessary to implement legally binding Union acts'	
Role of national parliaments	**Art 12 TEU** made it clear that national parliaments must actively contribute to the good functioning of the EU. **Protocol No 2** provided detail in regard to their role in the enactment of EU legislation	National parliaments required to be consulted in regard to new legislation, in order to ensure compliance with the principles of subsidiarity and proportionality
EU Membership	**Art 49 TEU** set out provisions relating to new members. **Art 50 TEU**, for first time, provided a procedure for the voluntary withdrawal of an MS from the EU	
Sharing of competences (power) between EU and its MS (subsidiarity & proportionality)	**Art 5 TEU** confirmed that EU may only act within the powers conferred by MS. Furthermore, **TFEU** distinguished between three categories of explicit 'competences' (power to act), namely: **Art 3** – areas of exclusive EU competence; **Art 4** – areas of shared competence; **Art 6** – areas where MSs have competence but may be 'supported' by EU	ToL clarified how power and roles were to be shared. Areas not in the 'threefold classification' lie within the exclusive competence of the MS. **Protocol No 2** provided further detail on the application of the principles of subsidiarity & proportionality. EU given new competences in areas such as climate change, sport, energy, IP, humanitarian aid and civil protection
The Institutions of the EU	**Art 13 TEU** increased the number of EU Institutions from 5 to 7. **Arts 13 to 19 TEU** clarify their roles, while **Arts 223 to 287 TFEU** set out details in regard to composition, functions etc.	European Council and ECB became Institutions. The role of elected EC President also created. Re-configuration of QMV in the Council in 2014. The EP capped at 750 members. The European Court of Justice renamed the Court of the European Union. The Court of First Instance renamed the General Court

(Continued)

Area of change/ Development	Overview of Change	Additional Notes
Future amendment of the Treaties	**Art 48 TEU** provided that the Treaties may, in future, be amended in two ways: the 'ordinary revision procedure' and the 'simplified revision procedure'	Details of the procedures for future revision of the Treaties set out in **Art 48 TEU**
Legal Acts of the Union (legislative procedures)	**Art 289 TFEU** provided that legislative acts (regulations, directives etc. (**Art 288 TFEU**)) could now be enacted under a process known as the 'ordinary legislative procedure' (previously the 'co-decision' procedure' (**Art 294 TFEU**)). The TFEU also provided for 'special legislative procedures' (**Arts 289 & 294 TFEU**)	The 'ordinary' legislative procedure became the usual procedure for enacting EU legislation, increasing the legislative power of the European Parliament
Enforcement of EU law	**Art 258 TFEU** – Actions to annul acts (ex Art 230 TEC); **Art 267 TFEU** – Preliminary References/ Rulings (ex Art 234 TEC); & **Arts 258/259/260 TFEU** – actions brought against MS (ex Arts 226/227/228 TEC)	Changes introduced in regard to whose acts can be challenged and also in regard to the circumstances of a challenge. Some change to language but not necessarily substance. Change to the process/ penalties relating to action against an MS (**Art 260 TFEU**) also introduced
Citizenship	**Art 24 TFEU** introduced citizens' 'right of initiative'	EU citizens given the power to propose EU laws to the European Commission. At least one million citizens 'who are nationals of a significant number of Member States' may take the initiative of inviting the European Commission to submit any proposal within the limits of EU powers

Democracy	**Arts 9 to 12 TEU** contain provisions relating to democracy. National parliaments are given a role in the 'policing' of subsidiarity	TEU now explicitly required the EU to respect **representative and participatory** democracy and the Institutions & other bodies to carry out their tasks in a **transparent** manner **(Art 15 TFEU)**
Fundamental/ Human Rights	**Charter of Fundamental Rights of the EU** becomes legally binding. **Art 6 TEU** provides the authority for the EU to accede to European Convention on Human Rights and Freedoms	Charter introduced in 2000 but originally persuasive only. Accession to the ECHR is thought not to affect the Union's competences as defined in the Treaties

III. THE EU TODAY

It should be evident by this stage that the EU is a complex structure. The Member States, while subscribing to the idea of an integrated Europe, do not always agree on the exact extent of such integration or on the means by which it should be achieved, and the issue of subsidiarity – or how competences are divided between the Member States and the EU Institutions – continues to be a major issue. The *original* community, the ECSC, created in 1952, was designed as a first step in achieving lasting peace and increasing prosperity in a continent scarred by war. These aims have, by and large, been achieved: half a century of peace together with the status of being one of the three most prosperous areas of the world are surely achievements to be proud of. However, the aims and objectives of the Union are constantly developing in response to both internal and external stimuli and the integration of Europe is far from complete.

The recent enlargement of the Union has itself presented significant challenges. The ambitious target of introducing a single currency throughout the Union continues to present a challenge. In addition, a further deepening of European integration to include both wider political and social issues presents yet further challenges. Add to this the Union's attempts at establishing a global identity and your head is likely to be left reeling with the enormity of the tasks which lie ahead for Europe!

Important dates and events in the creation of the EU:

Apr 1951   Six States sign the Treaty of Paris establishing the ECSC

Mar 1957   The six sign the Treaties of Rome establishing EURATOM and the EEC (in force Jan 1958)

Apr 1965   Merger Treaty is signed providing all three Communities with the same institutional structure

Apr 1970   First Budgetary Treaty signed, making major changes to the funding of the Communities

Jan 1973   Denmark, Ireland and the United Kingdom join the Communities

Dec 1974   Agreement on direct elections to the EP – a major step in ensuring a democratic Europe

Jul 1975   Second Budgetary Treaty signed

Jul 1978   European Council agrees on closer monetary co-operation

Jun 1979   First direct elections to the EP

Jan 1981   Greece joins the Communities

Jan 1986   Spain and Portugal join the Communities

Feb 1986   SEA signed with the aim of speeding up European integration (in force July 1987)

Feb 1992   TEU signed in Maastricht – creating the European Union (in force Nov 1993)

Jan 1995   Austria, Finland and Sweden join the Union

Oct 1997   ToA signed – consolidating Treaty aimed at enlargement & bringing EU closer to its citizens (in force May 1999)

Dec 2000   ToN signed. Main thrust was the reform of the Institutions in preparation for further enlargement (in force Feb 2003)

May 2004   Estonia, the Czech Republic, Latvia, Lithuania, Hungary, Poland, Slovenia, Slovakia, Cyprus and Malta join the EU

Jan 2007   Romania and Bulgaria join the EU

Oct 2004   Representatives of the 25 Member States sign the Treaty establishing a Constitution for Europe

May 2005   France and Holland reject the text of the Constitutional Treaty (finally abandoned during summer 2007)

Dec 2007   Representatives of the 27 Member States sign the Reform Treaty (now called the Treaty of Lisbon – ToL)

Dec 2009   ToL enters into force, amending the Maastricht Treaty (TEU) and amending and renaming the TEC – now Treaty on the Functioning of the European Union (TFEU)

SOME ISSUES TO THINK ABOUT FURTHER:

- Why was an integrated Europe seen as 'necessary'? What overarching aims were all three communities intended to achieve?
- What was the primary aim or emphasis of the original EEC? Did its short-term goals differ from its long-term goals?
- Why has it been necessary to 'develop' the European Communities/Union?
- What do you see as the main priorities for the EU in the future?

3 Who Runs the EU?

I. POWER SHARING

Since the first European Community (the ECSC) was created, the Member States have delegated various powers to a number of Institutions that have organised the 'running' of the Communities on their behalf. Together, these Institutions fulfil the main **functions of government** of the Union, taking decisions, creating laws and spending money on a joint (Union) basis – but *only* in areas in which they have been provided with the authority to do so. (This is known as the principle of *'conferral'* which is now set out in Art 4 TEU. The areas in which the Union may involve itself are detailed in Arts 3 to 6 TFEU.) The Member States still retain power to create and amend constitutional and substantive rules of the EU, as has been done through a variety of Treaties, already discussed in Chapter 2, and of course the Member States continue to be solely responsible in areas that lie outside the competence of the EU.

Over the years, numerous theories have been put forward in an attempt to explain how power is, or should be, shared between the Member States and its Institutions and, consequently, the way in which power is divided – and amongst whom – is the main focus of this chapter.

1. Federalism, supranationalism and intergovernmentalism

There is no precise, agreed definition of federalism and a cursory examination of various federal systems throughout the world reveals that there are numerous different models. However, in its most basic form, **federalism** can be concluded as being the dispersal of power between different levels of government. Federalism has proved a tremendous influence on the governance of the EU and, as we will see, power within the EU is shared not only between Union (institutional) and Member State (national) levels but also at regional and local levels, under the concept known as subsidiarity (discussed below). However, the question needs to be asked as to *how* power is shared between these various actors and consequently an understanding of the theories of supranationalism and intergovernmentalism becomes important.

Supranationalism occurs where the power to take decisions is concentrated at a level *above* that of participating States. As already touched upon, the Member States of the EU have created a number of Institutions which have been given various powers that allow them to 'run' the Union. Decisions taken by the Union's Institutions often take precedence over those taken by individual Member States, and so the Institutions can be concluded as having supranational authority.

Intergovernmentalism, on the other hand, occurs where participating States retain the power to take decisions, normally through unanimity, which subsequently allows each State to maintain significant control over decision making. Within the European Union, while the Member States have devolved power to the Institutions, they have also retained ultimate power for themselves, in that they have preserved the power to create and amend constitutional and substantive rules of the EU. The EU can therefore be said to also demonstrate intergovernmental tendencies.

Consequently, it can be concluded that governance of the EU displays a mix of both supranationalism and intergovernmentalism.

2. The division of competences (power) between the EU and its Member States

If it can be agreed that the power to govern the EU is shared, it becomes relevant to consider exactly *how* such power is apportioned. Before there can be *any* European Union involvement in a particular area, the Member States must have conferred power on the Union: for example, before the Institutions could become involved in the running of its Member States' coal and steel industries, the Member States must first have provided them with the authority to do so – which they did through agreeing the ECSC Treaty. Once such authority has been given, it then needs to be considered exactly how the Institutions and States divide power between them. Basically, what we need to ponder is:

(a) when can the Institutions act without the need to obtain the 'permission' of the Member States;

(b) when can the Member States act without reference to the Institutions; and

(c) when should the Institutions and States act together?

The Treaty on the Functioning of the European Union (TFEU), in particular Arts 2 to 6, refers to this as the allocation of 'competence'. The Treaty goes on to provide that there are three types of 'competence':

- First, there is **'exclusive competence'**. Exclusive competence relates to specific areas where *only* the Union Institutions may act (that is, take decisions which have legal impact).

- Second, there is **'shared competence'**. While this may appear to relate to specific areas where the Member States and the Union may both act, or come together to act, the situation is not as straightforward as it may first seem, as the Member States may *only* act in these areas *if* the Union has:

  - not yet exercised its right to act, or

  - decided to *cease* exercising its right to act.

  Exactly when the Union should exercise, or cease to exercise, its right to act and when it should allow the Member States to act is governed by two important principles: *subsidiarity* and *proportionality*, which are discussed in more detail below.

- Finally, there are specific areas where the Member States are afforded the right to act but where the Union reserves the right to **'support, co-ordinate or supplement'** the acts of its Member States.

This division of competences is set out under Title I of the TFEU (entitled Categories and Areas of Union Competence), in particular Art 2 TFEU, which details each form of 'competence'. Further, Art 3 TFEU lists the *specific areas* in which the Union has exclusive competence, while Art 4 TFEU lists the areas in which the Union 'shares' competence with its Member States. Article 6 TFEU sets out the areas in which the Union has competence to 'support, co-ordinate or supplement' the acts of the States. However, the Treaty also sets out a number of areas which do not fall into any of these three areas of competence: for example, Art 5 TFEU sets out areas in which the Union may *'co-ordinate policies'* or *'take initiatives'*. As this may be difficult to digest at first, you are strongly encouraged to carefully read Arts 2 to 6 TFEU, which should assist in consolidating your understanding of power sharing within the EU.

3. The principles of subsidiarity and proportionality

Article 5 TEU provides that the 'competences' discussed above are governed by two principles – those of subsidiarity and proportionality.

Specifically, the TEU states that in areas which do **not** come within the **exclusive** competence of the Union, the Union (through its Institutions) may **only** act if the objective(s) of any proposed action **cannot be effectively achieved** at national level (be that central, regional or local), **and** those objectives can be **better** achieved when action is taken at Union level.

This is the principle of *subsidiarity*. The principle can be seen as a means of avoiding over-centralisation and of ensuring that decisions are taken as closely as possible to the citizens of the EU, thus, hopefully, bringing the EU and its citizens 'closer together'. It is not a new principle and was first articulated by the Court of Justice of the EU as a General Principle of Union law (further discussed in Chapter 4) and, in 1993, given formal recognition by the Maastricht Treaty (TEU).

An alleged breach of the principle can result in a request for review being brought before the Court of Justice (Art 263 TFEU), although the Court has appeared reluctant to consider the principle in any real depth, as consideration of Cases C-233/94 and C-491/01, *Germany v European Parliament & Council* (the Tobacco Advertising Cases) demonstrate.

In terms of the legislative processes of the Union, the utility of the principle is reinforced by Protocol (No 2) on the Application of the Principles of Subsidiarity and Proportionality, which has been annexed to the TEU and TFEU by the Treaty of Lisbon. In particular, before proposing new legislation, the Commission is required to 'consult widely', taking into consideration the national implications of any such legislation. In addition, any draft act must be 'justified' by means of a statement demonstrating that both principles are being satisfied.

Significantly, the Protocol places national parliaments in the position of 'guardians' of the principle of subsidiarity, providing a procedure under which the parliaments may require a draft to be reviewed where its adherence to the principle is questioned. (Chapter 4 provides further detail on EU legislative procedures.) In addition, under jurisdiction afforded to it by Art 263 TFEU, the Court of Justice may also review the validity of legislative acts on grounds that there has been an infringement of the principle of subsidiarity. (Chapter 6 provides further detail in regard to this procedure.)

As already touched upon, Art 5 TEU also discusses the principle of *proportionality* in regard to the exercise of Union competences. In particular, it provides that Union action must not exceed what is **necessary** to achieve the objectives of the Treaties. Again, the principle was first developed by the Court of Justice as a General Principle of Union law.

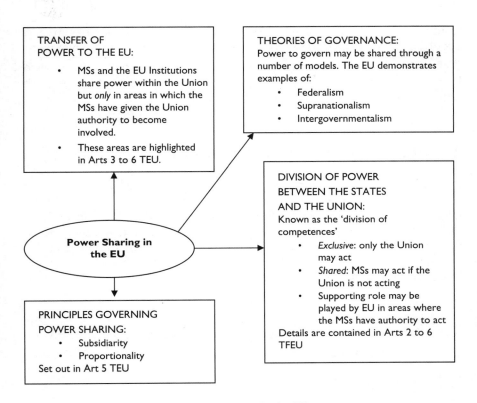

Power Sharing in the EU

II. THE INSTITUTIONAL STRUCTURE OF THE EU

1. The Institutions and other Union bodies

Article 13 TEU provides that the tasks entrusted to the Union shall be carried out by seven Institutions, namely the European Parliament (EP), the European Council (EC), the Council, the European Commission, the Court of Justice of the European Union, the European Central Bank (ECB) and the Court of Auditors (CoA). The Treaties have established several additional bodies such as the Economic and Social Committee (ESC) and

Committee of Regions (CoR). As the Communities have grown and developed into the EU, so too have the Institutions grown and developed.

In order to understand the workings of the Union's Institutions, each will be considered separately in terms of the role that it plays and also with regard to its relationship with the other Institutions.

2. The functions of government

It is worth taking a moment to consider the traditional division of the functions of government, that is: legislative, executive and judicial. In the UK, for example, each area is fulfilled by separate bodies, in order to check the potential for arbitrary government. No such division is attempted in Europe and the roles of government are shared, rather than divided, amongst the Institutions. It is not possible, therefore, to declare any single Institution as, for example, the legislator of the EU.

3. The European Parliament (Art 14 TEU and Arts 223 to 234 TFEU)

i. Composition and functions

The EP (or Assembly, as it was originally known) was created by the ECSC Treaty in 1952. It consisted of 78 members who were delegates nominated by the national parliaments. While the role of a parliament traditionally involves a substantial legislative function, the EP's legislative role was initially very limited, providing little more than a forum for debate.

Today the EP may be composed of a maximum of 750 members (known as MEPs), plus a President. Since 1979 the Parliament has, importantly, been directly elected through democratic elections held every five years in each Member State. It is the largest multinational parliament in the world, presently representing the interests of approximately 500 million EU citizens. It has no permanent home and sits in Strasbourg for monthly plenary sessions, holds committee meetings and additional sessions in Brussels, while its General Secretariat is based in Luxembourg. All of the EU's major political parties are represented in the EP, and MEPs are grouped together according to their political affiliations, rather than by nationality.

It is important to remember that, due to its democratically elected status, the European Parliament represents the interests of the citizens of the European Union.

ii. The legislative role of the EP

The process of enacting legally binding acts within the EU normally involves three of the EU's Institutions: the Commission, whose role is largely that of initiator (and drafter) of legislation (although the EP may request the Commission to submit proposals under Art 225 TFEU); the Council, which must normally provide its assent before legislation can take effect; and the Parliament, whose role has been rather varied over the years. Initially, the legislative role of the EP was extremely limited and largely confined to a process known as *'consultation'*. This procedure required that, before legislation could be adopted, the EP was to be consulted. While neither the Council nor the Commission was required to act on any opinions or proposals for change put forward by the EP, failure to consult could lead to legislation being declared void by the Court of Justice (Case 138/79, *Roquette Frères v Council*).

However, since the introduction of direct elections to the Parliament, the legislative power of the EP has grown significantly. The Single European Act 1986 (SEA) introduced a process known as *co-operation*, which was seen as a first step in the extension of the powers of the democratically elected Parliament. Under this procedure, the EP was able to 'reject' draft legislation, which the Council was subsequently only able to adopt by unanimous agreement (the decision-making process known as 'unanimity'), rather than the more usual qualified majority voting (QMV is a system in which votes are weighted to reflect the population of a State). While not placing the EP on an equal footing with the Council in terms of the legislative power, the procedure increased Parliament's influence, resulting in both the Council and the Commission becoming more inclined to take into consideration the EP's point of view. It should be remembered, however, that following the SEA, the consultation procedure was still very much the norm and that the new co-operation procedure was limited in its application to relatively few areas.

The TEU further increased the EP's legislative powers by introducing a procedure known as *'co-decision'*. The main difference between the co-decision and co-operation procedures was that the former allowed the EP to veto, by absolute majority, a proposed legislative measure. The importance of the procedure from the Parliament's point of view was that it allowed the EP to prevent the Council from passing legislation without its agreement. It is important to note, however, that the use of the co-decision was again limited, the co-operation procedure becoming the norm under the Maastricht Treaty. The Treaty of Amsterdam and the Treaty of Nice both extended the use of co-decision, which again had the effect of increasing the influence of the EP in the Union's legislative process.

Under the changes introduced by the Treaty of Lisbon the consultation procedure remains – but its use is extremely limited – while the use of the co-operation procedure has been discontinued. In addition, Art 289 TFEU provides that legislation can now be adopted by a procedure known as the *'ordinary'* legislative procedure, which is virtually identical to the co-decision procedure, which maintains the EP's status as 'co-legislator' with the Council. A further procedure, known as the *'special'* legislative procedure, has also been introduced by Art 289 TFEU. Both procedures are discussed in further detail in Chapter 4, as is the final legislative procedure, known as the *'consent'* (formally *'assent'*) procedure, which again is a rarely used procedure, under which the EP must provide its assent by majority.

iii. The budgetary role of the EP

Initially, the EP had, in line with its other legislative powers, a purely consultative role in relation to the Community's budget. In 1970, major changes were made with regard to the funding of the Communities and this coincided with the first major extension of the EP's powers through the 1970 and 1975 Budgetary Treaties.

Four Institutions have a part to play in the Union's budgetary process. The Commission is responsible for drawing up a draft budget, which the Council and Parliament may adopt, while the Court of Auditors (CoA) provides an annual audit of spending. A draft budget will contain details of proposed compulsory and non-compulsory expenditure and also an estimate of revenue. Prior to the introduction of the Treaty of Lisbon, the Parliament had the power to amend the sections of the budget relating to non-compulsory expenditure only. However, under Art 314 TFEU, the EP's power was extended to include amendments to both parts of the budget. Where the draft budget cannot be agreed by the Parliament and the Council a conciliation committee will be set up in order to achieve a consensus. If the EP and the Council decide to reject the draft budget, the Commission will be required to re-submit its draft.

iv. The EP's supervisory role

As there is no strict separation of powers within the EU, the Treaties provide for a number of 'checks and balances' which are intended to ensure that no one Institution becomes too powerful. As part of this system, the Institutions all play a part in supervising each other, and one of the more important supervisory powers held by the EP is that which it has over the Commission. The EP is entitled to ask questions of the Commission and demand written answers (Art 230 TFEU) and since 1973 the Parliament has made time in its schedule for a regular 'question time' with regard to the work of both the Commission and the Council. (While this power may be effective as a means of exposing wrongdoing, the Council, unlike the Commission, cannot be forced to reply to the EP's questioning.) The EP also debates, in open session, the Annual Report produced by the Commission.

The EP also has the authority to require the Commission to resign *en bloc* (Arts 17 TEU and 234 TFEU). This power has, to date, never been used, probably because it has been seen as rather severe and, it is also argued, in most circumstances the EP and the Commission consider themselves allies rather than adversaries. Also, until amendments were introduced by the Maastricht Treaty, the EP was unable to exert control over the appointment of new Commissioners and it would therefore have been rather pointless to sack the Commission when it had no control over who was to replace the outgoing Commissioners. New Commissioners must now, however, be approved by the EP before taking up office (Art 17 TEU).

The EP may exert supervisory powers over the acts of the other Institutions by instituting a legal challenge before the Court of Justice. This procedure, known as 'action to annul' or 'judicial review' (Art 263 TFEU, discussed in Chapter 6), provides that the Parliament may challenge any act which has legal impact produced by the other Institutions. It may similarly, under Art 265 TFEU, challenge the other Institutions should they *fail to act* when bound to do so by Union rules. It was originally thought that the Parliament lacked *locus standi* to make a challenge (as can be evidenced by Case 302/87, *European Parliament v Council*, the *Comitology* case). However, in the later *Chernobyl* case (Case C-70/88, *European Parliament v Council*), the Court declared that the Parliament might bring such an action in circumstances where it was acting to protect its 'prerogatives'. The EEC Treaty was later amended by the SEA to formally acknowledge this right, and the Treaty of Nice (ToN) increased the EP's role, which is now comparable to that of the Commission and the Council.

The EP also has supervisory powers in respect of allegations of maladministration: it may set up temporary Committees of Inquiry (Art 226 TFEU) to investigate such allegations – which may result from a complaint made by a citizen under Art 227 TFEU – and also elect a European Ombudsman to receive complaints regarding possible maladministration against any EU body (Art 228 TFEU). At the conclusion of an investigation the Ombudsman is required to report to the EP, which has no powers to correct the situation, but the process allows such maladministration to be brought to the attention of the media.

v. Conclusions

The Parliament, although initially weak, has been provided with substantially increased powers over time, largely as a result of its being directly and democratically elected. It can be argued that this is only right and proper, as it is the EP which enjoys the mandate of the peoples of Europe, and to continue to deny the Parliament a proper voice in Europe would have been to ignore the concept of democracy.

4. The European Council (Arts 15 to 16 TEU and Arts 235 to 236 TFEU)

Firstly, it should be emphasised that you should take care not to confuse the European Council with either the Council (of the EU) or the Council of Europe (which exists *outside* the EU).

i. Composition and functions

Initially, the European Council (EC) was an informal body, composed of the Heads of Government or State of the Member States, assisted by their Foreign Ministers, along with the President of the Commission. Their ad hoc meetings, known as summits, were formally recognised by the SEA, which required that the EC meets at least twice per year. Since the coming into force of the Treaty of Lisbon, summits must now take place twice every six months. The Treaty of Lisbon also made other significant changes, providing that the EC be recognised as a Union Institution (Art 13 TEU). It has been endowed with its own elected President (Art 15 TEU), which provides that the High Representative of the Union for Foreign Affairs and Security Policy also take part in its work. The EC has its base in Brussels.

The Maastricht Treaty (TEU) gave the EC a defined, if rather vague, role as providing the Union with 'the necessary impetus for its development' and providing that it 'shall define the general political guidelines thereof'. The body has fulfilled an important role in reaching agreement between the Member States where there has been a failure to reach consensus at a lower level. It is also involved in the ratification of agreements (which must normally be reached by consensus: Art 15 TEU). It was agreement at EC level that led to the introduction of direct elections for the EP and also to the creation of a European unit of currency, while the impetus for the creation of a European Union (following on from the European Communities) was a result of an ad hoc committee set up by the European

Council (the Dooge Committee), while major changes to the various Treaties have been preceded by summit meetings which, in turn, have led on to intergovernmental conferences (IGCs) from which amendments to primary legislation have emerged.

ii. Conclusions

The European Council can be seen as an important force within the EU, developing policy and providing direction.

5. The Council (Art 16 TEU and Arts 237 to 243 TFEU)

i. Composition and functions

Formerly referred to as the Council of Ministers and, following the Maastricht Treaty, the Council of the European Union, the Council is comprised of one representative from each Member State authorised to bind the government of that State. The composition of the Council has always been dependent on the subject matter under discussion: for example, if the Council is discussing matters relating to agriculture, each State's agriculture minister, or equivalent, will be present. Similarly, if transport matters are under discussion, transport ministers will be in attendance. Article 19 TEU develops this, providing for the Council to meet in 'different configurations', with a General Affairs Council ensuring the consistency of the work of each 'configuration'. In addition, a Foreign Affairs Council 'shall elaborate the Union's external action', on the basis of guidelines set out by the European Council (EC). The Foreign Affairs Council is presided over by the High Representative of the Union for Foreign Affairs and Security Policy, who is an EC appointee. The Council's 'configurations', other than the Foreign Affairs Council, are led by a team of presidents, again appointed by the EC. It is the presidencies that decide what is discussed and when.

The Council is supported by a Committee of Permanent Representatives of the Governments of the Member States (known collectively as COREPER), which is responsible for 'preparing' the work of the Council (Art 16 TEU). COREPER consists of senior diplomats and it is instructive to note that it has been suggested that anything up to 90 per cent of all Council decisions are actually taken by COREPER before they even reach ministerial level! In addition to COREPER, the Council also has a General Secretariat providing administrative support.

The Council represents national interests and, as a body, has characteristics of both a supranational and intergovernmental organisation. The ministers who form the Council are responsible to their national parliaments, yet they form part of the institutional body that makes decisions on behalf of the European Union. The TFEU provides that 'the Council shall, jointly with the European Parliament, exercise legislative and budgetary functions. It shall carry out policy-making and co-ordinating functions as laid down in the Treaties'.

The Council, along with the European Council, represents the interests of the governments of the Member States.

ii. The legislative role of the Council

Originally, the Council was considered to be the principal legislator for the Communities. Following developments wrought by the amending Treaties, the Council now shares its legislative role with the European Parliament, with whom it also shares budgetary powers.

The main legislative procedure of the Union, through which the majority of legislative acts are now enacted, is known as the *ordinary legislative procedure*, as set out in Art 294 TFEU. Under this procedure, the Commission will submit a draft legislative proposal to both the Council and the EP and, in summary, if the two Institutions fail to reach agreement on the content of the proposal it will be abandoned, thus denying the Council the opportunity to push through legislation without the EP's approval, as it once could. While other legislative procedures exist, known as *special* legislative procedures, these are limited to particular circumstances, as set out by the Treaties. (Further details on the Union's legislative procedures are provided in Chapter 4.)

iii. Decision making in the Council

In addition to its legislative powers, the Council sets political objectives, co-ordinates national policies and provides a forum where differences between the Member States may be resolved. When the Council is required to reach a decision – whether it relates to legislation or another matter – it does so by taking a vote. There are three systems of voting that may be used: simple majority, qualified majority or unanimity. Reaching a decision by simple majority requires that the majority of Council ministers support a proposal. This requires Member States to surrender a high degree of sovereignty and is consequently rarely used.

Initially, the favoured method of voting was unanimity, effectively allowing each Member State the power of veto. While this method is still used in very restricted areas, QMV has become the norm. (Art 16 TEU). Under this method, each Member State's vote is 'weighted' to reflect the size of its population and this method of reaching decisions means that a State may find itself bound by a decision which it does not approve of. When, in 1966, the Council moved towards the regular use of QMV, France refused to attend Council meetings (known as the 'empty chair' policy), objecting to the resulting loss of sovereignty. This protest resulted in what has become known as the *Luxembourg Compromise* (or Accords), when it was agreed that, should a decision be required on an issue relating to 'very important interests' of a Member State, that State would be treated as having a right of veto. This had the effect of increasing the power of the Council, which represents Member State interests, and decreasing the influence of the Commission, which represents the interests of the Community as a whole. The effect of this 'veto' should not be overemphasised, however, as it has never been recognised as having legal effect, although it has clearly encouraged the Member States to reach agreement through compromise whenever possible.

Presently, under QMV, a decision must normally receive at least 255 votes and be approved by the majority of the Member States. In addition, any member of the Council may request verification that the qualified majority represents at least 62 per cent of the total population of the EU. Articles 16 TEU & 238 TFEU provide that from 1 November 2014 a change will be introduced in regard to the 'formula' for QMV. Normally, any decision will require at least 55 per cent of the Council, representing at least 65 per cent of the EU population, to approve a measure, while a 'blocking minority' is also defined by the Treaty Article.

iv. The other roles of the Council

In terms of the budget, the Council shares its role with the EP under a process which has already been set out above. The Council also co-ordinates the general economic policies of the Member States, while, in addition, the Council, in the same manner as the EP, exerts supervisory powers over the other Institutions by virtue of the judicial review procedures contained in the TFEU. This procedure, also known as 'action to annul' (Art 263 TFEU), is discussed further in Chapter 6.

v. Conclusions

Given its composition, it is clear that the **Council represents the interests of the governments of the Member States**, resolving issues of conflict and playing an important role in developing legislation.

6. The Commission (Art 17 TEU and Arts 244 to 250 TFEU)

Once known as the 'High Authority', the Commission's position within the institutional balance of the Community has varied considerably during its lifetime, fluctuating between being heralded as the embryonic European Government and a less auspicious Community civil service. The Commission's position within the institutional balance has undoubtedly suffered as a result of the increased power enjoyed by the EP, and the 'Brussels bureaucrats' are seen as being held in low esteem by the general public – at least if the UK's popular press are to be believed – and publicity surrounding the Commission's en bloc resignation in 1999, as a result of allegations of malpractice, did little to improve its reputation. On the whole, however, the Commission can be seen as a success, as the progress made with regard to European integration could not have been achieved without the Institution's input as motivator, monitor and negotiator.

The Commission represents the interests of the European Union as a whole.

i. The composition of the Commission

The Commission is comprised of 27 individuals, one from each Member State, who are appointed for a renewable period of five years. Commissioners, who must be EU citizens, are appointed under a procedure involving the Council, the President of the Commission and the EP. The TFEU requires that each Commissioner be independent, not take instruction from any government or other body and act only in the interests of the Union. While a Commissioner who fails to fulfil the conditions of his/her appointment may be required to resign by the President of the Commission, the EP may also dismiss the Commission en bloc.

The membership of the Commission includes its President and the High Representative of the Union for Foreign Affairs and Security Policy. After first consulting the EP, the European Council proposes a President from amongst the Commissioners, who must then be formally elected by the EP. This is a particularly influential post, as the President will not only chair Commission meetings and attend the meetings of the European Council, but will also represent Europe at international summits. The High Representative is also proposed by the European Council and, in order to take up their role in the Commission as a Vice President, the High Representative has to appear before Parliament for questioning and is then subject to Parliament's vote of approval on the proposed Commission.

ii. The functions of the Commission

While the EP represents the interests of the citizens of Europe and the Council represents the interests of the Member States, the Commission represents the interests of the Union as a whole. And this is reflected by Article 17 TFEU which provides that the Commission must 'promote the general interests of the Union and take appropriate initiatives to that end'.

The Commission is divided into directorates-general (DGs), each headed by a director-general who in turn reports to a Commissioner with overall responsibility for the work of that DG. The DGs are divided by subject matter, for example, industry or matters relating to education, training and youth. Each Commissioner is supported by a cabinet and the Commission has a total staff of approximately 25,000.

The Commission is a multi-purpose organisation and its functions include the legislative, executive and quasi-judicial functions as outlined below.

iii. The Commission's legislative role

The Commission plays a central role in the Union's legislative process, its most important function being that of initiator of draft legislation. As has already been discussed above in relation to the EP, the Commission will produce draft legislation which it then sends to the Council and the EP for their consideration and/or approval. The Commission further participates in the legislative process by amending legislative proposals in circumstances where either the Council or Parliament or both have failed to provide the necessary agreement, often reacting to amendments suggested by those Institutions.

Many of the Commission's proposals for legislation are a direct result of Council requests that various studies be undertaken and the EP may also request that the Commission submits legislative proposals on appropriate matters. The Commission publishes an annual programme outlining its legislative plans and listing legislative priorities for that year, thereby playing a part in planning the strategy for the Union as a whole. In addition, the Commission has been dubbed the 'motor for integration', due to its involvement in the development of policy. This can be evidenced, for example, by the Commission's White Paper entitled Completion of the Internal Market (COM (85) 310), which was significant in the shaping of the SEA.

The Commission also has the power, in very limited circumstances, to act alone in the making of EC legislation. In addition, the Council may delegate legislative powers to the Commission, once again in limited circumstances.

41

iv. The Commission's administrative and executive roles

Legislation, once enacted, must be implemented and policy, once made, must be put into effect. The Commission's role is generally not one of direct action, as both policy and legislation are largely put into effect at national level, but to maintain a supervisory position, ensuring that the appropriate Member States' agencies comply. The Commission manages the EU's annual budget, including a number of funds such as the European Social Fund and, importantly, the European Agricultural and Guarantee Fund, which takes up a large proportion of the Union's annual budget.

The Commission also has a central role with regard to the Union's external relations. The EU's effectiveness on a global level is enhanced by the Commission's role as negotiator of trade and co-operation agreements with countries or groups of countries outside the Union. The Commission, for example, represents the EU at the United Nations and its specialised agencies, such as the World Trade Organization.

v. The Commission's supervisory functions

The Commission has a number of supervisory (or quasi-judicial) functions. First, Art 258 TFEU provides the Commission with the power to investigate, and bring before the Court of Justice, any Member State that it considers to be in breach of its Union obligations. The Commission attempts to encourage States to remedy a breach as informally as possible, through consultation and negotiation and an action before the Court is seen very much as a last resort. (This action is discussed in further detail in Chapter 6.)

Second, the Commission plays an important role in ensuring that Union rules relating to competition are followed. For example, any undertaking (the favoured EC term for a firm or individual capable of economic activity) that attempts to distort trade within the Union may find itself in breach of EU law. Under Regulation 17 (1956–62 OJ Spec Ed 87), the Commission was provided with the power to investigate possible breaches, provide formal decisions as to whether there has been an infringement and impose fines against any wrongdoers, a power which it now shares with appropriate bodies within the Member States. While the investigative and forensic powers of the Commission may be subject to judicial review, these functions provide the Commission with significant influence in relation to the development of EU policy.

In addition, the Commission, in the same manner as the other Institutions, exerts supervisory powers over the other Institutions by virtue of annulment procedures contained within the Treaty (discussed in Chapter 6).

vi. Conclusions

It can be concluded that the Commission's functions elevate it far above that of a 'civil service' for the Communities/Union. It can be described as a *sui generis*, multi-functional organisation with not inconsiderable influence over not only the day-to-day running of the Union, but also its development and direction. This said, its powers are not boundless and many are held under the discretion of the Council and the supervision of the EP.

7. The Court of Justice of the European Union (Art 19 TEU and Arts 251 to 281 TFEU)

The European Union is founded on the rule of law and acceptance by the Member States, Union bodies and individuals of the binding nature of its 'rules' is fundamental to the Union's existence. Originally, the Court was known as the European Court of Justice. In November 1989, a Court of First Instance (CFI) was created to assist the Court in its tasks. The Court of Justice of the European Union, as it has been known since the coming into force of the Treaty of Lisbon, is now made up of the Court of Justice (the Court), the General Court (GC, previously the CFI) and 'specialised courts'. The Courts sit in Luxembourg.

Although the rules of precedent do not apply to the Court, in reality the Court has, for the sake of consistency, tended to follow its past decisions. An infrequent example of the Court failing to follow its past judgments can be evidenced in the *Keck* judgment (Cases C-267 and 268/91 which is discussed in Chapter 7).

i. The composition of the Court of Justice

The Courts are made up of a number of personnel including judges and advocate-generals (AGs), while each court also has a President and a Registrar. While the judges act as decision makers, AGs, who have no equivalent in the UK's legal system, assist the judges by delivering non-binding written opinions, which provide advice to the Court prior to their deliberations.

The number of judges composing the *Court of Justice* is dependent on the number of Member States: one judge per State, for a period of six years, renewable every three years. Both the TEU and TFEU emphasise that judges be 'persons whose independence is beyond doubt', and it is clear that judges must be independent of any government or interest group. As with all fixed-term appointments, it is possible that political pressure could be brought to bear on judges. The likelihood of this is reduced, however, as the Court's deliberations are secret, with a single ruling being delivered by the Court rather than individual judgments from each judge.

With regard to the qualifications, the TFEU requires that judges must be individuals who 'possess the qualifications required for appointment to the highest judicial offices in their respective countries or who are jurisconsults of recognised competence' (TFEU). While the UK has so far chosen to appoint domestic judges or legal practitioners, the Treaty allows academics to be appointed, and a number of other States have done so. In addition, the Court has eight AGs, with the rules of appointment and qualifications being the same as those for judges. All appointments are made by the Member States, following consultations with former Court judges.

The number of judges in the *General Court* must also include at least one judge from each Member State but this number may be increased (Art 254 TFEU). The General Court is also assisted by AGs.

ii. The functions and jurisdiction of the Court of Justice

Article 220 TEC set out the role of the Court of Justice rather succinctly by providing that it was to 'ensure that in the interpretation and application of this Treaty the law is observed'. The TFEU now provides the Court's jurisdiction. The various actions that can be brought before the Court can be divided into direct actions and preliminary rulings. Direct actions include those brought by the Commission against Member States accused of failing to fulfil their EU obligations, and actions brought by the Institutions or individuals wishing to challenge the validity of legally binding acts of the EU (both are discussed in further detail in Chapter 6).

Preliminary rulings, on the other hand, are the result of requests by national courts requiring the Courts to either interpret EU law or rule on its validity. National courts will make such requests when they have a case before them that revolves on a point of Union law (again, see Chapter 6).

In addition to its specific jurisdiction, the Treaty provides that the Court has the rather general function of ensuring the 'law is observed'.

iii. Judicial activism and the Court's interpretive methods

It has been argued that the Court of Justice has used its rather broad remit to expand its role beyond that normally performed by a judicial body. The Court has adopted a purposive, teleological or contextual, rather than literal, approach to interpreting EU law. As it explained in Case 283/81, *CILFIT*: 'Every provision of Community law must be placed in its context and interpreted in the light of the provisions of Community law as a whole, regard being given to the objectives thereof.' This has allowed the Court to take a major role in filling gaps left by Union legislation which, in turn, has resulted in its being accused of usurping the role of both the Union legislators and policy makers.

Such activism has been denied by both the Court and its supporters, who argue that the Court of Justice has gone no further than was necessary to give effect to the Treaty, given its nature, which is intended to be no more than a framework.

It cannot be denied that the Court has produced some particularly dynamic decisions and one has to look no further than Case 26/62, *Van Gend en Loos*, to see the impact that the Court has had on the development of Union law (discussed in Chapter 5). It has been argued, however, that the Court is now playing a far less proactive role, perhaps now content that the Union legal order has been adequately developed. (Although its activism in the development of protection of Fundamental Rights within the Union, further discussed in Chapter 4, may belie this.)

iv. Procedure before the Court

Procedure before the Court can be divided into two stages – oral and written. Unlike the UK, however, emphasis is placed on written submissions rather than oral, which are limited and short (which is probably advantageous as the case may be heard in any of the Union's official languages).

The written stage comes first, with relevant documents being communicated to all parties and published in the Official Journal of the European Union. At the end of the written stage, cases may be argued orally in open court and it is following this hearing that the AG will deliver his opinion.

The judges, who may sit in plenary session (all judges) or in chambers, deliberate behind closed doors, delivering their judgment in open court. The judgment, which will be made available in all official languages, will include the reasoning on which it is based. (It is worth noting that the AG's opinion is often very instructive and worth reading.)

v. The General Court

The General Court (GC), originally known as the CFI, was established under the SEA as a means of relieving the excessive workload of the European Court of Justice. The jurisdiction of the Court is set out under Art 256 TFEU, which is similar to the jurisdiction of the Court of Justice; appeals from the GC are to the Court of Justice.

vi. Conclusions

The importance of the Court in the development of the Union's legal system is well recognised. It is generally accepted that the Court has succeeded in constitutionalising the Treaties by articulating the relationship between the EU and its Member States and also between EU law and national legal systems. It has achieved this by putting 'flesh on the bones' of the Treaties and developing understanding of Union law and how it should be applied.

8. The European Central Bank (Arts 282 to 284 TFEU)

The European Central Bank (ECB) was created by the TEU (1992) and is now an Institution of the EU. It has been tasked with administrating the monetary policy of the Member States that have the euro as their currency (i.e. the 'Eurozone'). The ECB, together with the national central banks, make up the European System of Central Banks (ESCB).

The main role of the ECB is to maintain price stability within the Eurozone by ensuring that inflation is kept as low as possible. In addition it defines and implements monetary policy, controls foreign reserves and issues euro banknotes. It also works with national and international banking systems to maintain a stable financial system. The ECB enacts legislation in order to fulfil its functions and, in a similar manner as the other Institutions, exerts supervisory powers over the other Institutions by virtue of annulment procedures contained within the Treaty (discussed in Chapter 6).

9. The Court of Auditors (Arts 285 to 287 TFEU)

The Court which, confusingly, is not a court at all as it has no judicial functions, was established by the Budgetary Treaty 1975, but it was not until the TEU (1992) came into effect that it was afforded the status of Union Institution. It is comprised of one member from each Member State. Both the Council and EP are involved in the appointment procedure and auditors must be appropriately qualified and their independence beyond doubt.

The CoA can be described as the 'taxpayer's representative', a 'watchdog' over the EU's money and, as the Union's budget has increased, so has the prominence of the Court, although it still remains 'low-key' compared to the other main Institutions. Every Institution and body that has access to Union funds is subject to the scrutiny of the CoA and the Court provides a check that all legal requirements are observed and also that the Union is receiving value for money.

The CoA publishes an annual report, highlighting any areas where improvements are possible or desirable. The Court also provides the EP and the Council with a Statement of Assurance, which declares that EU money has been spent for the purposes intended.

10. Other Community bodies

The EU Treaties also make provision for a number of other bodies, the main ones of which will be considered very briefly:

i. The Economic and Social Committee (Arts 300 to 304 TFEU)

The Economic and Social Committee (ESC) is a consultative body which represents a variety of sectional interests. Its membership consists of up to 350 representatives drawn from a broad cross-section of European society, such as workers, employees, farmers, craftsmen, professionals, consumer groups and so on. Meetings are held on a monthly basis.

The TFEU requires that draft legislation, in specific policy areas, be referred to the Committee and that the majority of new Union laws of any significance are adopted only following input from the ESC.

ii. The Committee of Regions (Arts 300 and 305 to 307 TFEU)

The Committee of Regions (CoR) was established by the TEU (1992) to represent regional and local interests. Like the ESC, it has a membership of up to 350, drawn from around the Member States, and must be consulted by the Council and Commission where the Treaty so specifies.

As national barriers break down and borders between the Member States become more open as a consequence of the internal market, the creation of a CoR can be seen as a response to people's fears over centralisation. The CoR has direct experience of how EU policies affect the everyday life of citizens and its expertise allows it to bring a powerful influence to bear.

iii. European Investment Bank (Arts 308 to 309 TFEU)

The European Investment Bank (EIB), whose membership comprises the Member States, is the EU's financing Institution, providing long-term

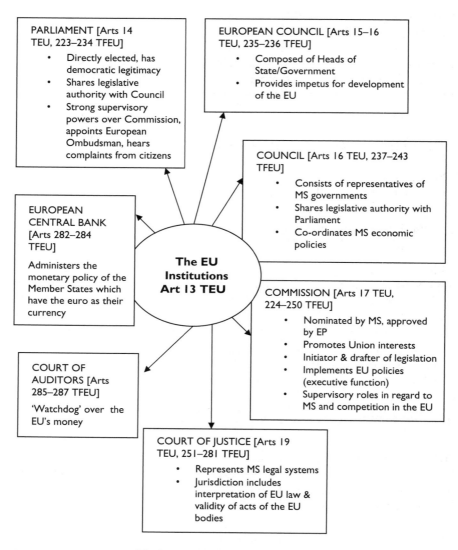

The Institutional Structure of the EU

loans for capital investments which promote the Union's economic development and integration. It supports regional development and its loans are often accompanied by grants from the EU's Structural and Cohesion Funds.

III. INSTITUTIONAL BALANCE, ACCOUNTABILITY AND DEMOCRACY IN THE EU

1. Institutional balance

As already discussed above, power within the EU is shared between (a) Member States and (b) bodies which have been set up to perform Union functions (basically the Institutions). In addition to considering power sharing between the Member States and the Institutions, it is also important to consider how the Institutions share the power afforded to them.

As has been previously highlighted, the Institutions of the EU represent different interests: the European Parliament represents the interests of European citizens, the Council represents the Member States' interests, in particular the governments of those States, while the Commission represents the interests of Europe as a whole. Consequently, it is vital that the powers and influence of these Institutions are carefully balanced in order that no one Institution – or the interests which they represent – becomes too powerful, overshadowing the interests of the other groups.

Originally, the powers of the Council and the Commission dwarfed those of the Parliament. In terms of legislative power, for example, the EP's role was mainly that of debating legislative proposals, with little opportunity to exert significant control over what did, or did not, become law. The original, effectively subordinate, role of the EP can also be further evidenced by consideration of the supervisory procedure known as 'action to annul' or 'judicial review' (Art 263 TFEU, discussed further in Chapter 6) under which the Parliament, unlike the Commission and Council, was unable to challenge the validity of the acts of the other Institutions.

However, the growth in the Parliament's powers has been considerable over the years. Following the introduction of direct elections to the EP in 1979, the authority of the Institution has increased with every subsequent amending Treaty. As already discussed above, its legislative powers were increased by the SEA and successive Treaties have further developed these powers with new legislative procedures such as the co-operation procedure and the co-decision procedure eventually giving it a right of veto over legislation in certain areas. The changes resulting from the Treaty of Lisbon further expanded Parliament's role as co-legislator with the Council, as the co-decision procedure – renamed the 'ordinary legislative procedure' by the Treaty (Art 289 TFEU) – has become the default procedure for the majority of EU legislation. Similarly, in respect of the EP's supervisory role, the Parliament is now on a par with the Commission and Council in terms of its ability to challenge the acts of other Institutions under Art 263 TFEU. The Union's budgetary procedures, again discussed above in terms of the EP's role, have further increased the EP's power over the years and it now enjoys parity with the Council in this area also. Similarly, the EP's influence has increased through its supervisory role over the Commission.

However, as power is finite, it should be remembered that as the EP's role has increased, the power of the other main Institutions has been somewhat reduced as a result. The Council is no longer the main legislator of the EU, nor does it have sole power to give assent to all areas of the Union's budget. Similarly, due to the Commission being subject to the supervisory powers of the Parliament, its influence has also been kept in check, thus ensuring that no one Institution has the potential to exert inappropriate influence within the EU.

2. Legitimacy, accountability and democracy in the EU

The issues of legitimacy of the European Union, the accountability of its Institutions and democratic standards within the EU are inextricably linked. As already explained above, the Institutions fulfil the main functions of government within the European Union. These functions are shared amongst the Institutions and, in order to remove the potential for arbitrary government, not only do the powers enjoyed by the Institutions have to be divided – or balanced – appropriately but accountability of the Institutions is also fundamental to the legitimacy of the EU. Similarly, the accountability of those who take decisions is fundamental to the issue of democracy within the Union.

Democracy, in its simplest form, can be loosely defined as government by the people, usually through elected representatives (which is known as 'representative democracy' and on which the Union is founded (Art 10 TEU)). In terms of the EU this was seen as problematic as, originally, none of the EU Institutions was *directly* elected by its citizens – the Parliament and Commission were nominated by the Member States and the Council, although composed of ministers, was still considered rather distant from the electorate. Added to this was the complaint that the Institutions lacked transparency, taking decisions out of the public eye, thus reducing their accountability. Consequently, a common complaint was that Europe suffered from a 'democratic deficit'.

The EU has, however, worked hard to reduce this 'deficit'. In terms of the Institutions, direct election of MEPs was seen as enormously significant, with the powers of the Parliament being appreciably extended to reflect their mandate, as has already been highlighted above. Decision making in the Council has also become more democratic, with the introduction and increased use of qualified majority voting (QMV), under which each Member State's voting capacity is determined largely by the size of its population. In addition, the accountability of the Union Institutions has been extended through increased transparency in terms of decision making: for example, EU documents are now far more accessible, while the development of the principle of subsidiarity, also already considered above, has reduced the possibility of illegitimate expansion of the Institutions' powers.

The Treaty of Lisbon further emphasised the importance of democracy by setting out the democratic principles on which the EU is based (Arts 9–12 TEU), highlighting not only that the Union is founded on representative democracy but that every citizen has the right to participate in the democratic life of the Union (participative democracy). In particular, in terms of leadership of the EU, the EP and Council gain more influence over the Commission through the process of appointing the Commission President. In terms of legislation, the influence of the EP is once more

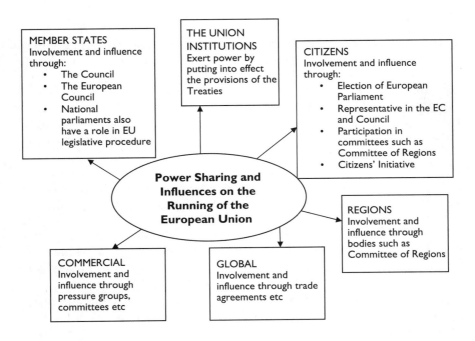

Influences on the Running of the EU

increased, as the use of the 'ordinary' legislative procedure (formally the co-decision procedure) is extended to new areas, while the use of QMV is similarly extended. Transparency is improved in the Council, as meetings involving debate on legislation are held in public, allowing national governments to more effectively supervise their representatives.

Some commentators have argued that the Union should not be required to achieve democracy as is expected within Member States, due to the nature of the decisions taken within the EU, the lack of interest shown by its citizens in electing their European representatives and also because accountability can be achieved though other means (for example, through the checks and balances built into the Treaty, such as judicial review, adherence to the principles of subsidiarity, proportionality and respect for Fundamental Rights and so on, all of which are discussed in further detail elsewhere). However, as the Union continues to expand and move into new areas of competence it would appear that improving democracy, accountability and therefore legitimacy is still a priority.

IV. CONCLUSIONS

Once the Member States took the decision to organise the Communities (now Union) in a manner which involved the creation of Institutions to 'run' Europe on their behalf and carry out the day-to-day functions of government, it has been important to clarify who would 'staff' these bodies, how roles would be allocated to and between them, and also how far their powers should extend. These issues are important because they strongly impact on democracy and accountability in the EU and, consequently, its legitimacy.

When attempting to understand – and memorise – the roles of the Institutions, it is helpful to think of them in terms of the traditional roles of government; that is, legislative, executive and judicial (or quasi-judicial). Similarly, it is also important not to forget that the main Institutions all represent different interests – those of European citizens (the EP), the Member States (the Council) and European interests as a whole (the Commission) – which should be helpful when trying to understand why it is so important that no single body becomes too powerful.

It is also essential to understand that the Member States, while allocating power to the Institutions, are the ultimate authorities in terms of the EU. Consequently, the allocation of competences between the States and their Institutions is a priority. While the Institutions may be tempted to allow their powers to 'creep' into areas which have been reserved for the Member States, it's important to understand how the Treaties ensure that this is not allowed to happen!

SOME ISSUES TO THINK ABOUT FURTHER:

- There are a number of theories of governance: which apply to the EU and how?
- How, and on what basis, are powers within the EU distributed between the Member States and its Institutions?
- How, and on what basis, are powers distributed between the EU's Institutions?
- What does the term 'democracy' mean to you? Is the EU 'democratic'? Does it need to be, given its limited competences?
- What does the term 'subsidiarity' mean in terms of European governance? What does the TFEU have to say about the principle of subsidiarity?

4 Sources of Union Law

In order to develop an understanding of European Union law, its main sources need to be examined. EU law can be divided into two basic categories: primary and secondary. The primary source of EU law is the various Treaties, both those that were enacted in order to create the original European Communities and also those that have been enacted in order to *amend* the original Treaties. (An overview of such Treaties is provided in Chapter 2.) The Treaties provide a framework of policies and rules, which are then fleshed out by the other sources of law.

Secondary sources include secondary legislation, as enacted by the Institutions of the Union, case law, which comes from the judgments of the Court of Justice, general principles as 'declared' by the Court and international agreements entered into by the Union. Each of these sources will be considered in turn.

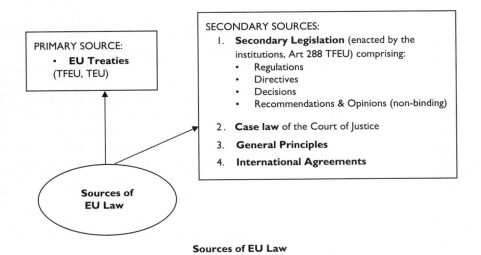

Sources of EU Law

I. PRIMARY SOURCES OF EU LAW

Three separate Treaties originally created three separate European Communities, namely:

- the Treaty Establishing the European Coal and Steel Community, 1951 (commonly called the Treaty of Paris or the ECSC Treaty);

- the Treaty Establishing the European Atomic Energy Community, 1957 (also called the *First* Treaty of Rome or the EURATOM Treaty); and

- the Treaty Establishing the European Economic Community, 1957 (also called the Treaty of Rome or EEC Treaty and *renamed* the Treaty Establishing the European Community (TEC) by the Treaty on European Union (TEU) and more recently the Treaty on the Functioning of the European Union (TFEU) by the Treaty of Lisbon).

In addition, the Treaty on European Union, 1992 (also called the Maastricht Treaty or the TEU) created the overarching European Union in 1993.

The most important Treaties from the point of view of the European Union today are, of course, the TFEU and the TEU, as they are the Treaties which set out a framework on which the Union is based. (Note that the dates given for the various treaties are the years in which they were signed, rather than the years in which they came into effect, which normally differ.)

There have also been a number of Treaties enacted which have not provided 'stand alone' law but which have **amended** the EEC/TEC/ TFEU and TEU, including the Merger Treaty 1965; the Budgetary Treaties 1970 and 1975; the Single European Act (SEA) 1986; the Treaty on European Union[1] (TEU) 1992 (also known as the Maastricht Treaty); the Treaty of Amsterdam (ToA) 1997; the Treaty of Nice (ToN) 2000; and the Treaty of Lisbon 2007 (originally known as the Reform Treaty).

The Treaties, along with secondary legislation, are divided into 'articles', which are basically the same as 'sections' in UK legislation. They can be written thus: Art 249 TFEU, with the last few letters demonstrating which Treaty the article is contained in. It is important to remember that in the 'hierarchy' of Union law the Treaties sit at the top and should always be the first source consulted when researching EU law.

---

1 It should be noted that the TEU could be included in either list as not only did it amend the then EC Treaty, but it also created the EU.

1. Creating primary legislation

The Member States hold the ultimate authority to develop and amend Treaties. Under procedures recently refined by the Treaty of Lisbon, an amendment to the Treaties (i.e. the TEU or TFEU) may be introduced by one of two legislative procedures: the Ordinary Revision Procedure or the Simplified Revision Procedure, both of which are set out in **Art 48 TEU**.

In outline, under the **Ordinary Revision Procedure**, a Member State, the European Parliament (EP) or the Commission may initiate the procedure by submitting a proposal for amendment to the Council, who will then notify the Member States of the proposal and submit it to the European Council (EC). The EC may then convene a Convention, composed of representatives of national parliaments, Heads of State, the EP and the Commission, to consider the proposal. Alternatively, should the EC, together with the EP, feel that a Convention is not necessary, the proposal can be put before an intergovernmental conference (IGC) comprised of representatives of the Member States. Before any amendment can come into effect, it must be ratified by the Member States in a manner that accords with their constitutions. Once ratified, the amendments will come into effect on an agreed date. If not all States have ratified but, after two years, a minimum of four-fifths of the States have ratified the amendment, the matter must once more be referred to the EC.

However, should an amendment proposal relate to Part Three of the TFEU (which relates to Union Policies and Internal Actions, seen as a 'less sensitive' area), the **Simplified Revision Procedure** may be used. In outline, under this procedure the EC may adopt an amendment, normally by unanimity, after consulting with the EP and Commission (and ECB, if in regard to a monetary issue). The EC must notify the Member States of the proposed amendment and, if no opposition to the amendment is voiced within six months, the EC may adopt the amendment provided the agreement of the EP is also given.

II. SECONDARY SOURCES OF EU LAW

1. Secondary legislation

Article 288 TFEU provides that: 'To exercise the Union's competences, the Institutions shall adopt regulations, directives, decisions, recommendations and opinions.'

Learning Resources

i. Regulations

Article 288 TFEU further provides that: 'A regulation shall have general application. It shall be binding in its entirety and directly applicable in all Member States.'

The fact that regulations have 'general application' and are 'binding in their entirety' means that they will be effective *throughout* the EU, on every Member State and in full. Regulations must be published in the Official Journal (Glossary) and come into force on the date specified by the regulation or, if no such date is specified, on the 20th day following publication.

'Direct applicability' means that regulations automatically take effect in each Member State *without the need for national implementing measures*. The Court of Justice has gone as far as to provide that Member States must not pass any incorporating measures (Case 34/73, *Variola*), as this could result in a Member State placing its own interpretation on the legislation.

Regulations achieve uniformity of law throughout the EU.

ii. Directives

Article 288 TFEU provides that: 'A directive shall be binding, as to the result to be achieved, upon each Member State to which it is addressed, but shall leave to the national authorities the choice of form and methods.'

Directives differ from regulations in a number of ways. They do not have general application and so do not have to be addressed to *all* Member States. Additionally, they are not directly applicable and, normally, the rights and obligations created by them only become effective when they have been incorporated into national law by the appropriate national authorities. They do, however, place an obligation on Member States to ensure that a particular aim is achieved by a particular date, leaving national authorities to decide on the exact implementation details. This allows a far greater degree of flexibility, providing Member States with the opportunity to introduce a measure in the manner best suited to each State.

Directives are often the chosen method where harmonisation, rather than uniformity, of law is the aim.

iii. Decisions

Article 288 TFEU provides that: 'A decision shall be binding in its entirety. A decision which specifies those to whom it is addressed shall be binding only on them.'

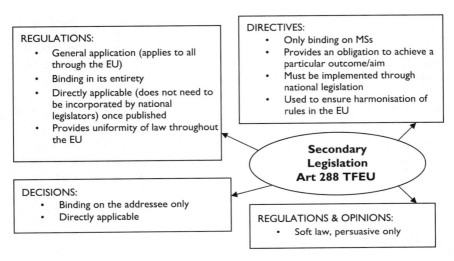

Secondary Legislation in the EU

A decision is similar to a regulation in that it has direct applicability, requiring no national implementation in order to take effect. All decisions must be published in the Official Journal, taking effect on a prescribed date or on the 20th day following publication.

iv. Recommendations, opinions and 'soft' law

Unlike regulations, directives and decisions, recommendations and opinions are not legally binding.

Article 288 TFEU provides that they have 'no binding force', although they are persuasive and should be taken into account by national courts (Case C-322/88, *Grimaldi*). Such sources of law are sometimes known as 'soft law'. Other sources of soft law may include guidelines or codes of conduct issued by the Union's Institutions.

2. Enacting secondary legislation

All binding secondary legislation is subject to review by the Court of Justice, which may adjudicate on its validity. It is particularly important that the correct procedures are followed when creating such legislation, as failure to do so may render the legislation invalid. (Judicial review of legally enforceable acts of the Institutions is further discussed in Chapter 6.)

i. The main actors in the enactment of secondary legislation

The enactment of secondary legislation normally involves four groups: the Commission who take responsibility for initiating and drafting new legislative proposals, the European Parliament and the Council, whose assent is normally required before legislation can come into effect and, finally, national parliaments who consider legislative proposals in order to ensure that they comply with the principle of subsidiarity.

In addition, a number of other groups may be involved in the process, for example, in certain circumstances the ECB may adopt legislative acts, while the Union's advisory bodies such as the Economic and Social Committee may be involved in a consultative capacity.

The roles of the main bodies is discussed further, below.

ii. The legal base for the creation of secondary legislation

European legislators must demonstrate that they have the necessary authority to enact secondary legislation. Such authority will derive from Treaty articles empowering the Institutions to legislate and is known as the 'legal base'.

The choice of legal base will depend on the subject matter of the proposed legislation. If, for example, the EU wishes to legislate on the free movement of workers, the legal 'authority' for doing so is provided by Art 46 TFEU. However, should the EU wish to enact secondary legislation in relation to taxation, Art 113 TFEU provides authority to do so. Where no such specific law-making powers are provided, Art 352 TFEU may provide a general power to legislate.

All secondary legislation should contain a statement as to the legal basis on which it is based and it is vitally important that the correct legal base is used, as the validity of the legislation will be open to challenge under the judicial review procedure (Chapter 6) if the wrong base is used. An example of this can be found in Case C-376/98, *Germany v Parliament & Council* (*'Tobacco Advertising' Case*) where the legal base used to enact Directive 98/43/EC (which imposed a general ban on tobacco advertising) was given as Art 114 TFEU (then Art 95 TEC). The Court of Justice held that the incorrect legal base had been used and the Directive was consequently declared void.

iii. Legislative procedures

Before looking at the specific procedures under which secondary legislation may be enacted, it is important to briefly consider the need for collaboration between all interested parties, both in the planning of legislative strategies and in regard to the content of new acts. Consultation and co-operation between various parties allows the interests of Member States, citizens, the Union as a whole and a variety of pressure groups to be taken into consideration and is essential to ensure the democratic nature of the decision-making processes within the Union. It should therefore be understood that the whole issue of law making may be far more complex than first appears. Not only do the competing interests of the Institutions have to be balanced, but also the competing interests of the various groups within the Institutions, such as the various Member States, political parties and so on.

The Union's legislative process has tended to be complicated, providing a number of different procedures by which secondary legislation may be enacted. This has been due, in the main, to additional procedures being developed over the years in order to increase the legislative power of the European Parliament, a point already touched upon in Chapter 3.

The question of *which* legislative procedure should be followed in any one set of circumstances is answered by the legal base. For example, if the Union wishes to enact legislation relating to the free movement of workers the legal base (Art 46 TFEU) will be the decisive feature, rather than the form that the legislation is to take – the procedure will not differ if a directive were to be proposed rather than a regulation.

The main, or 'default', legislative procedure is the 'Ordinary' legislative procedure, while 'Special' legislative procedures include a 'Consultation' procedure, a 'Consent' procedure, the 'Council and Commission acting alone' and the 'Commission acting alone'. Each is discussed in outline below.

The 'ordinary' procedure (Arts 289 and 294 TFEU)

This procedure, originally known as the 'Co-decision' procedure prior to the enactment of the Treaty of Lisbon, was introduced by the TEU to enhance the legislative power of the EP. The complex procedure, which is now the main legislative procedure by which Union acts are adopted, involves the Commission sending a legislative proposal to both the Council and the EP. If both the Council and the EP approve the proposal, it will be adopted.

Should consensus not be reached, this signals the beginning of a stage whereby the proposal may be subject to a 'to-ing and fro-ing' between the Council and EP. If agreement still cannot be reached, a Conciliation Committee will be convened by the Commission in an attempt to draw up a joint text which is acceptable to both the EP and Council. If this cannot be achieved within six weeks of the Committee being convened, the proposal will fail. If a joint text is agreed, it will again be put before both Institutions for their approval.

'Special' legislative procedures (Arts 289 and 294 TFEU)

'Special' legislative procedures relate to specific circumstances highlighted by the Treaties, where the 'Ordinary' procedure need not be followed.

The Commission acting alone

This method is rarely used and it is sufficient to say that it involves the Commission acting without intervention from the other Community Institutions. An example of the use of this procedure may be found under Art 106 TFEU, which allows the Commission to address directives or decisions to Member States.

The Commission also enjoys delegated legislative power. Although not strictly a legislative procedure, the Council may, through parent legislation, authorise the Commission to enact regulations in specific areas such as agriculture and competition; this allows legislation to be enacted quickly in areas that are highly regulated.

The Council and Commission acting alone

Here the Council may adopt a proposal from the Commission without having to refer to any other authority. An example of this procedure may be found under Art 31 TFEU, which allows the Council to fix Common Customs Tariffs, following a proposal from the Commission.

The 'Consultation' Procedure

Under this procedure, which was found in the original EEC Treaty, the Commission may put forward a proposal to the Council who, in turn, must consult the EP. No obligation is placed on either the Council or the Commission to follow the EP's opinion, however, although the resulting legislation may be annulled should the EP not be consulted (Case 138/79, *Roquette Frères v Council*).

An example of the Consultation Procedure can be found under Art 22 TFEU, in regard to the rights of EU citizens.

The 'Assent' Procedure

In a small number of areas, the positive approval of the EP is required before the Council can adopt a proposal. This procedure, originally introduced by the SEA, affords the EP an absolute power of rejection. An example of its use can be found under Art 177 TFEU.

While it is important to get to grips with the procedures by which the Union's Institutions may enact secondary legislation, there is far more to the legislative process than mere procedure.

3. Voting procedures

When Institutions have to take legislative decisions, the voting procedures adopted are of significance as different options available can impact on the influence exerted by participants. The various voting methods available to the Institutions are as follows:

- *Simple majority:* Under this procedure each participant (but not those who are absent) is given a single vote and a decision is reached on the basis of the largest number of votes received. An argument against this voting method is that the rights of the minority may be sidelined. This is a method through which the **Commission** reaches its decisions.

- *Absolute majority:* This method requires that over half of all those with a vote (including any absentees) must agree before a proposal can be carried. Majority voting is the method adopted by the **European Parliament** (Art 231 TFEU), although whether it be by simple or absolute majority will depend on the specific requirements of the Treaty.

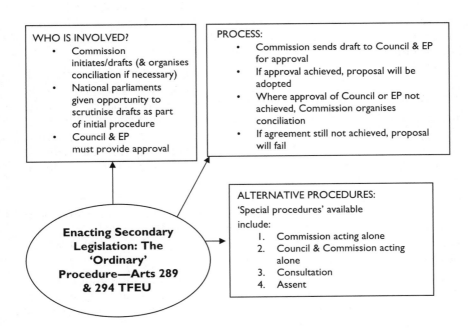

WHO IS INVOLVED?
- Commission initiates/drafts (& organises conciliation if necessary)
- National parliaments given opportunity to scrutinise drafts as part of initial procedure
- Council & EP must provide approval

PROCESS:
- Commission sends draft to Council & EP for approval
- If approval achieved, proposal will be adopted
- Where approval of Council or EP not achieved, Commission organises conciliation
- If agreement still not achieved, proposal will fail

Enacting Secondary Legislation: The 'Ordinary' Procedure—Arts 289 & 294 TFEU

ALTERNATIVE PROCEDURES:
'Special procedures' available include:
1. Commission acting alone
2. Council & Commission acting alone
3. Consultation
4. Assent

Enacting Secondary Legislation in the EU

d majority (QMV): Here votes are weighted according to the population of each Member State. This form of voting is considered the most democratic and is the method under which the **Council** takes decisions, *unless* otherwise provided by the Treaties, and Art 238 TFEU should be consulted in terms of the exact workings of the procedure, which is due to be amended in November 2014.

- *Unanimity:* Before agreement can be reached under this procedure, all participants in the vote must agree. While this system demonstrates solidarity and unity amongst voters, it can also significantly increase the time taken to achieve agreement and so is limited in its use to issues of high importance. This method of voting also allows participants to 'veto' a decision.

III. CASE LAW OF THE COURT OF JUSTICE

The Court's function, as provided by Art 19 TEU, is to 'ensure that in the interpretation and application of the Treaties, the law is observed'. As the Treaties and secondary legislation are often imprecise or insufficiently comprehensive, this has provided the Court with the opportunity to significantly contribute to the corpus of Union law.

The importance of the Court's case law should not be underestimated. By virtue of its favoured purposive, or teleological, method of interpretation (use your Glossary!) – and its jurisdiction to provide preliminary rulings (discussed in Chapter 6) – the Court has, virtually single-handedly, developed the EU's legal system, constitutionalised the Treaties and filled in gaps in legislation. While there is no formal system of precedent, with the Court being free to depart from its own past decisions should it see fit, in the interest of consistency this has seldom occurred. (For an example of the Court departing from its past decisions, however, consider cases C-267 & 268/91, *Keck*, further discussed in Chapter 7.) With regard to the relationship between the Court's decisions and national courts, the Court's decisions *do* have a precedential value, as can be evidenced by the Court's dicta in Cases 28–30/62, *Da Costa* (discussed further in Chapter 6).

The case of *Van Gend en Loos* (Case 26/62) epitomises the importance of the case law of the Court of Justice, demonstrating the Court's approach to its role and also the extent of its impact. It is consequently *strongly* recommended that students read this judgment and consider its consequences. (The case is discussed in further detail in Chapter 5.)

IV. GENERAL PRINCIPLES OF UNION LAW

General principles of law, which can be found in all advanced legal systems, have the function of assisting where written sources of law are not sufficiently comprehensive. The General Principles of Union law have been developed by the Court of Justice and have been used to 'flesh out' the law found in the Treaties and secondary legislation.

General principles of Union law have been held to include equality, fundamental rights proportionality, subsidiarity and legal certainty, many of which have gone on to be formally recognised by inclusion in the Treaties.

1. The function and status of general principles

General principles have been used by the Court to assist in the interpretation of European legislation and also as a factor when considering the validity of secondary legislation (an example of which is Case 112/77, *Topfer v Commission*). In addition, they can provide a restraint on the activities of the Member States (for example, Case 11/70, *Internationale Handelsgesellschaft* IHG).

The Court has been creative in developing these principles, using the purposive method of interpretation and discovering them as 'threads' running through:

* the Treaties;
* the legal systems of the Member States;
* international law.

The Court of Justice has justified its actions by referring to three Treaty Articles which, it argues, give it the necessary authority, namely:

* Article 220 TEC (now Art 19 TEU), which provided that the Court shall 'ensure that in the interpretation of the Treaties the law is observed', the term 'law' in this context being understood to mean more than the written sources of law contained in the Treaties;
* Article 230 TEC (now Art 263 TFEU), which provided 'infringement of the Treaties or any rule of law relating to their application'. 'Any rule of law' in this context has been interpreted to be a reference to law other than that contained in the Treaties;

- Article 288 TEC (now Art 340 TFEU), which referred to 'general principles common to the laws of the Member States'.

In order to provide a flavour of how these principles have been developed and applied, a number of important examples will be considered in turn below. **It should, however, be noted that a number of General Principles originally articulated by the Court have now been formalised by incorporation to the Treaties.**

2. Equality – 'discovered' in the Treaties

The Treaties refer to the principle of equality on a number of occasions and is an example of the Court developing a general principle by bringing together 'threads' found in the Treaties.

While Art 12 TEC (now Art 18 TFEU) prohibited discrimination on the grounds of nationality, Art 34(2) TEC (now Art 40 TFEU) prohibited discrimination between producers or consumers within the EU. In addition, Art 141 TEC (now Art 157 TFEU) provided for equal pay between men and women, and the Court, on the basis of these 'threads', developed the more general principle of non-discrimination.

The Court went on to use the principle to prohibit discrimination based on grounds such as nationality (Case 293/83, *Gravier v City of Liège*) and gender (Cases 75a and 117/82, *Razzouk and Beydouin v Commission*).

The principle of equality or non-discrimination is now formally supported by the Treaties as the ToA introduced Art 13 TEC (now Arts 2 and 19 TFEU), which provided the EU with the authority to legislate in order to prohibit discrimination based on 'sex, racial or ethnic origin, religion or belief, disability, age or sexual orientation'.

3. Fundamental Rights – 'discovered' in national and international law

Although not mentioned in the three original (largely economic) Treaties, the Court of Justice, in cases such as Case 29/69, *Stauder v City of Ulm* and Case 11/70, *Internationale Handelsgesellschaft*, confirmed that rights guaranteed under (German) national law are also to be protected by what was then the European Economic Community. Similarly, the Court, in Case 36/75, *Rutili v Ministre de l'Interieur*, confirmed that rights found in the European Convention for the Protection of Human Rights and Fundamental Freedoms (ECHR) would be protected by the Court.

Once again the proactive approach of the Court appears to have been vindicated. The ToA amended the TEU (then Art 6 Maastricht Treaty, now Arts 2 and 6 TEU) which set out that the EU would respect fundamental rights. Later, the Union went further by drafting a Charter of Fundamental Rights, which was given legal status by the Treaty of Lisbon. In recognition

Overview of the Development of the Protection of Fundamental Rights in the European Union

---

Initially
- **Community Treaties fail to mention FR:** unsurprising as the Communities are largely economic in nature and protection already available under the European Convention on Human Rights (ECHR) created by the Council of Europe (non-EU body)
- **Court of Justice** supports this approach (Case 1/58, *Stork v High Authority*)

Change of Attitude
- **Court of Justice** explains that protection of FR is enshrined in the General Principles of EU law (based on the law of the MS and international treaties such as ECHR) (Case 26/29, *Stauder v Ulm*, Case 11/70, *Internationle Handelsgesellschaft (IHG)* and Case 4/73, *Nold*)
- **Member States** must also respect FR when implementing EU law (Case 5/88, *Wachauf*)

Support for the Court of Justice's position on FR
- **Joint Declaration** by the European Institutions in 1977
- FR referred to in amending **Treaties** (TEU 1992)

Impact of the ECHR on EU
- While Court of Justice recognises ECHR as a **source** of the EU General Principle of FR, Court provides that the ECHR does not bind the EU (then EC) and that the EC does not have the power to accede to the ECHR (*Opinion 2/94 on Accession*)
- TEU refers to ECHR

Charter of Fundamental Rights
- Drafted by EP in 2000. Charter was persuasive rather than binding
- Charter given **legal effect** by the Treaty of Lisbon and now has same weight as Treaties (Art 6 TEU)

The Future
- EU has been given the authority to accede to the ECHR (Art 6 TEU). What this will mean is somewhat uncertain as TEU also provides that accession will 'not affect the Union's competences'
- *The Protocol on the Application of the Charter of Fundamental Rights* also provides that nothing in the Charter creates rights applicable to the UK or Poland

---

of the importance that the principle has now assumed, a flowchart highlighting its development in a little more detail is set out on p 67. Not only does it aim to demonstrate the development of the principle but it also demonstrates the influence on EU law that can be exerted by the Court of Justice.

V. INTERNATIONAL AGREEMENTS

The EC was given legal personality under Art 281 TEC and was empowered by Art 300 TEC to enter into international agreements with third countries, which were recognised as an integral source of Community law. The EU now enjoys legal personality under Art 47 TEU, while Art 216 TFEU continues to provide that such international agreements concluded by the Union are binding on the Institutions and on its Member States.

VI. CONCLUSIONS

Union law is an evolving legal system, containing rules that provide rights, obligations and remedies. It has evolved over time and continues to develop in response to the needs and objectives of Europe. Contained in numerous sources, it is made up of rules which effectively provide the Union's constitution, direction on how the Union is to be administered and also the substantive law of the EU. Once this has been understood, the time is right to consider the relationship that exists between Union law and the law of its Member States.

SOME ISSUES TO THINK ABOUT FURTHER:

- Which of the EU Treaties were merely amending Treaties and which contain the principles and rules by which the EU is presently governed?

- How do the various sources of secondary legislation differ form one another?
- From what source do legislators obtain the necessary authority to enact secondary legislation? How is secondary legislation enacted? Is there a different procedure for each type of legislative act?
- What role(s) do the General Principles of EU law play?

5 The Relationship between Union Law and National Legal Systems

I. THE DOCTRINES OF DIRECT EFFECT AND SUPREMACY

The status of EU law within the legal systems of the various Member States is of fundamental importance, and there are a number of questions that must be answered before an understanding of Union law and its impact can be fully gained.

First, it is necessary to consider which source of law will take precedence should there be a conflict between EU law and national law. Second, it is necessary to consider the effect of EU law in the Member States, who receives rights and obligations under it and whether, where and how such rights may be enforced.

1. The original position

Surprisingly, the founding Treaties did not address these questions directly and the original Member States assumed that EEC law would have the same domestic effects as other sources of international law, resulting in the status of the EEC Treaty being determined by each Member State's own constitutional rules.

In dualist States (such as the United Kingdom), *international* law is only binding on individuals if it has been adopted by the national authorities and made part of domestic law. In such States, it was therefore considered that the EEC Treaty would not provide enforceable rights to citizens unless specifically incorporated.

On the other hand, in monist States (such as the Netherlands), once ratified, international law automatically forms part of the national legal system. In Member States with such constitutional rules, it was consequently assumed that EEC law automatically became part of that State's domestic legal system. As a result, the status – and impact – of EEC law varied from State to State.

The Court of Justice, however, took a different approach to the question of the impact of Community law and developed two principles, which later become known as the 'Twin Pillars upon which the Community rests', namely, direct effect and supremacy. Each will be considered in turn.

2. The doctrine of supremacy of Union law

Member States have two legal systems with which to contend – that containing national law and that of the EU. It therefore needs to be considered which source of law should be applied in cases of conflict between these two sources. As the Treaty is largely silent on this issue (although it may be implicit in a number of provisions) it has been left to the Court of Justice to provide guidance.

i. The creation of the doctrine of supremacy

While the Court did not address the issue of supremacy of European law directly in Case 26/62, *Van Gend en Loos (Van Gend)*, it explained that Community (now Union) law constitutes a 'new legal order ... for the benefit of which the States have limited their sovereign rights, albeit within limited fields'. The Court's judgment also resulted in Community law (what is now Art 34 TFEU) being applied, rather than the conflicting national (Dutch) law, which was set aside by the domestic court.

It is clear from the Court's dicta that it was recognised that to allow Member States to apply conflicting national law rather than Union law would severely undermine the ability of the EU to achieve its aims. Thus, the doctrine of the supremacy (or primacy) of Community law was established.

ii. The development of the doctrine

The precise implications of the doctrine of supremacy were not addressed until Case 6/64, *Costa v ENEL*. In this judgment the Court confirmed that where national law and EU law conflict, EU law must take precedence, even where the national law has been enacted subsequent to EU law, thus ruling out the possibility of national law taking precedence under the concept of 'implied repeal' (that is, a process recognised under UK law whereby later law will always be presumed to have automatically repealed any conflicting earlier enacted law).

The Court provided a number of arguments in support of its dicta. First, it confirmed that EU law is an integral part of domestic legal systems, also providing that Member States had created this new legal system by limiting their sovereign rights and transferring power to the EU.

Drawing heavily on the spirit and aims of the (then EEC) Treaty, the Court pointed out that the uniformity and effectiveness of Union law would be jeopardised should national law be allowed to take precedence. In addition, the Court argued that the obligations undertaken by the Member States would be 'merely contingent' rather than 'unconditional' if they could 'be called into question by subsequent [national] legal acts'.

The Court also referred directly to the text of the EEC Treaty to support its judgment. Although the original Treaties did not – and the TEU and TFEU still do not – provide directly for the supremacy of European law, the Court of Justice argued that Art 189 EEC (now Art 288 TFEU), which provides for the direct applicability of regulations, would be meaningless if Member States could negate their effect by enacting subsequent, conflicting legislation.

While *Van Gend* and *Costa* dealt with the theoretical principle of supremacy, the Court had little to say on the practical application of the concept. A serious threat to the supremacy of EU law was revealed in Case 11/70, *Internationale Handelsgesellschaft*, when the German Administrative Court voiced its concern over the legal foundations on which the principle of supremacy was based. The German Court's disquiet revolved around its concern that fundamental rights contained within the German constitution could be overruled by European law. The Court of Justice made it clear that EU law is supreme over *all* forms and sources of national law, softening the blow by declaring that the Union recognised such fundamental rights as an 'integral part of the general principles of law' whose protection would be ensured 'within the structure and objectives of the Community' (now Union).

In Case 106/77, *Amministrazione delle Finanze dello Stato v Simmenthal*, as a result of a preliminary reference, the Court of Justice was required to consider whether a national court should disapply conflicting national legislation, even in situations where that court had no domestic jurisdiction to do so (in Italy, this function was carried out by the Constitutional Court). The Court of Justice provided that where conflict arises between national and European law, the national court, under European law, is required to give immediate effect to EU law and not wait for a ruling from the Constitutional Court.

This judgment is important, in that it confers on domestic courts jurisdiction that they may not have under domestic law. Once more, the European Court emphasised the need for such action in order to ensure the effectiveness of Union law.

A further example of the jurisdiction of national courts being extended by Union law can be found in Case C-213/89, *R v Secretary of State for*

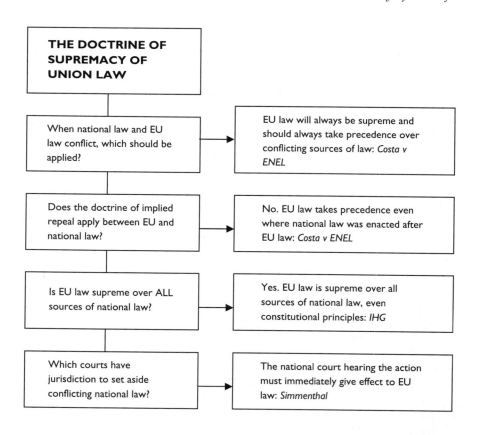

The Doctrine of Supremacy of EU Law

Transport ex p Factortame Ltd (Factortame (No 2)). In this case, the Court of Justice explained that a national rule must be set aside by the national court if that rule prevents the court from granting interim relief. This can be seen as an additional example of the practical consequences of the doctrine of supremacy.

3. The doctrine of direct effect of EU Law

i. The creation of the doctrine

The Court of Justice provided a ground-breaking judgment in Case 26/62, *Van Gend en Loos (Van Gend).* Van Gend had imported a quantity of chemicals from Germany into the Netherlands and was required, by Dutch law, to pay customs duty to the Dutch authorities. The importers challenged the legality of the duty, claiming that it was an infringement of Art 12 EEC (now Art 30 TFEU). The Dutch tribunal referred the question to the Court of Justice under the preliminary reference procedure (Art 267 TFEU, discussed in Chapter 6).

In order to arrive at its decision, the Court drew heavily on the purposive method of interpretation (look at the Glossary), relying not only on the wording of the Treaty, but also on the spirit and aims of the Community. In

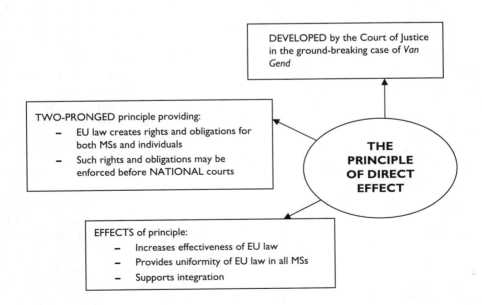

The Doctrine of Direct Effect of EU Law

its judgment, the Court declared that the Community constituted a new legal order of international law, which conferred both rights and obligations on individuals, as well as on the participating Member States, without the need for implementing legislation. The Court further concluded that national courts must protect such rights. In other words, the Court of Justice provided that EEC law (now EU law) had direct effect, which can be seen as a two-pronged concept under which:

- EU law provides not only Member States with rights and obligations, but individuals also; and

- such rights and obligations can be enforced by individuals before their national courts.

From this judgment, which was opposed by a number of Member States including the Netherlands and Belgium, it can be concluded that the Court was motivated by the need to ensure the integration, effectiveness and uniformity of European law.

ii. The conditions for direct effect

The Court explained in *Van Gend* that not all Treaty articles would be capable of direct effect and it is now clear that any provision must first fulfil a set of criteria if it is to have direct effect (these criteria will hereafter be called the *Van Gend* criteria, for ease of explanation). It should be noted that some sources may refer to the *'Reyners* criteria' after the case in which they were first listed together (in the AG's Opinion in the case). The *Van Gend* criteria require that in order to have direct effect, the legal provision must be:

- *clear and precise* – it is logical that if law is to be enforceable, both parties must be clear as to what their respective rights/obligations are. The Court of Justice has therefore declared that a provision must be 'sufficiently clear and precise' before being capable of direct effect. This does not necessarily mean that the whole provision must comply: in Case 43/75, *Defrenne v Sabena*, for example, it was held that only part of Art 119 EEC (now Art 157 TFEU) fulfilled this criterion but was consequently directly effective;

- *unconditional* – a provision will not be unconditional if the right it provides is in some way dependent on the judgment or discretion of an independent body unless that discretion is subject to judicial control (an example of this may be found in Case 41/74, *Van Duyn*);

- *not subject to any further implementing measures on the part of either the Union or national authority* – this criterion would appear to have been subject to rather liberal application by the Court, as can be demonstrated in Case 2/74, *Reyners*. In this case, based on the wording of the Treaty, it had been anticipated that secondary legislation would have to be enacted before the objectives contained in Art 52 EEC (now Art 49 TFEU) would provide rights to individuals. However, the Court declared the provision to be directly effective, explaining that to do otherwise could result in individuals being denied their EU law rights.

iii. Direct effect of the various sources of Union law

The doctrine of direct effect has been further developed and expanded upon over the years and the important developments are set out below.

Direct effect and Treaty articles

As we have already seen above, the question of whether the principle of direct effect applies to Treaty articles was considered in the judgment of *Van Gend en Loos* when Art 12 EEC (now Art 30 TFEU) was held to be directly effective.

It is now accepted that Treaty articles are capable of direct effect, *providing* that they comply with the three *Van Gend* criteria. In addition, the Court has provided that rights and obligations contained in Treaty articles may be enforced both against the State and public bodies (*vertical* direct effect: *Van Gend*) and against private bodies and individuals (*horizontal* direct effect: Case 43/75, *Defrenne v Sabena*).

Direct effect and regulations

Article 288 TFEU would appear to give regulations direct effect, providing as it does that a regulation 'shall be binding in its entirety and directly applicable in all Member States'. Direct applicability should be interpreted as meaning that a provision requires no implementation or further action by the Member States in order for it to take effect in national law. While all regulations (*and* Treaty articles) are directly applicable, the Court confirmed in Case 9/70, *Franz Grad*, that regulations would be directly effective only when able to fulfil ALL of the *Van Gend* criterion. As with Treaty articles, regulations may be enforced both vertically and horizontally.

Direct effect and decisions

Decisions, as regulations, are directly applicable, but Art 288 TFEU provides that they can be binding on those to whom they are addressed (whether that be Member States, corporations or individuals). The Court of Justice has held that decisions will be directly effective, providing they fulfil the *Van Gend* criteria, against an addressee (Case 9/70, *Franz Grad*).

Direct effect of international agreements

This is a controversial and complex area, outside the scope of this book. It is sufficient to conclude that in an attempt to ensure that Member States respect any commitments arising from such agreements, the Court has ruled that international agreements may have direct effect if the circumstances are appropriate (Case 104/81, *Kupferberg*).

Direct effect and directives

This has proved to be a particularly controversial area. Article 288 TFEU provides that: 'A directive shall be binding, as to the result to be achieved, upon each Member State to which it is addressed, but shall leave to the national authorities the choice of form and methods.'

Directives are therefore *not* directly applicable, as they require implementation into national law by a State's legislative body. Consequently, directives do not appear to provide rights to individuals until they are incorporated – and then through national incorporating legislation, rather than the directive itself – although they *do* place obligations on Member States.

Despite the wording of Art 288 TFEU, which would appear to preclude directives from being directly effective, the Court has held that where a directive has not been properly implemented into national law, it may still give rise to direct effects (*Franz Grad* and *Van Duyn*).

The Court has confirmed that in order for directives to be directly effective, they must satisfy the *Van Gend* criteria. While the first two criteria present few problems, it would appear that the final criterion is impossible to satisfy. However, once the date on which the directive *should* have been implemented has passed, the ECJ has shown itself willing to conclude that this criterion has also been satisfied (Case 148/78, *Pubblico Ministero v Ratti*).

The Court has argued that this approach makes directives both more effective and also stops Member States from relying on their own 'wrongdoing', should they fail to incorporate a directive into domestic law. This development has not been without its critics, however, who argue that to allow directives to be directly effective removes the distinction between regulations and directives.

In response to such criticism, the Court of Justice has explained that directives are distinct as they may only be enforced vertically (that is, against the State) and not horizontally (that is, against individuals) (Case 152/84, *Marshall v Southampton and South West Hampshire AHA (Marshall (No 1))*.

In the *Marshall* case, Miss Marshall wished to enforce rights emanating from the Equal Treatment Directive (Council Directive (76/207/EEC)) against her employer. She attempted to do this in the appropriate national court – an employment tribunal (ET). The ET made a preliminary reference to the ECJ (under Art 267 TFEU), asking whether she could rely on the directive. The Court replied that she could do so as she wished to rely on the provisions of the directive against the State, who were one and the same as her employers. In other words, she could rely on the vertical direct effect of the directive.

This requirement has the unfortunate effect of discriminating between individuals who wish to enforce their rights against a State, as compared to those wishing to pursue the same rights against an individual. The problem can be illustrated by consideration of Case 151/84, *Roberts v Tate & Lyle Industries* (the *Tate & Lyle* case), which mirrored the circumstances of *Marshall* (*No 1*). Ms Roberts also wished to enforce rights emanating from the Equal Treatment Directive but, as she was employed by a private corporation as opposed to an emanation of the State, her rights were unenforceable. The Court has further attempted to mitigate such discriminatory effects by providing a wide interpretation of 'State', as can be seen below.

4. Developing the effectiveness of directives

i. Vertical direct effect: a wide interpretation of 'State'

In an attempt to circumnavigate the problems highlighted above, the Court of Justice has shown itself willing to adopt the widest possible definition of 'State'.

As already discussed, the Court has been willing to recognise a Health Authority as part of the State, while in Case 103/88, *Fratelli Constanzo*, regional and local government were also considered to be within the definition. In Case 222/84, *Johnston v Chief Constable of the RUC*, the Chief Constable was also recognised as being an 'emanation of the State'.

In Case C-188/89, *Foster v British Gas*, the European Court provided some guidance by explaining that a directive may be relied upon against organisations or bodies which:

* have been made responsible for providing a public service, and/or
* are subject to the authority or control of the State, and/or
* have special powers beyond those which result from the normal rules applicable to relations between individuals.

These guidelines, while failing to provide an inclusive definition of 'State', have nevertheless proved helpful by making it clear that something *more* than mere control is necessary.

This conclusion is supported by the Court of Appeal's dicta in *Doughty v Rolls Royce* (1992). Although Rolls Royce was, at the time of the action, wholly owned by the British State, it was not considered an 'emanation of the State' as the company neither provided a public service nor had any of the 'special powers' referred to in *Foster*.

ii. Indirect effect or the 'interpretive obligation'

The Court of Justice's refusal to allow the horizontal direct effect of directives has without doubt lessened their effectiveness as legislative instruments. In an attempt at remedying this, the Court has developed a principle which has become known as 'indirect effect' or 'the interpretative obligation'.

The basic principle

In Case 14/83, *Von Colson*, the Court reminded Member States of their duty, provided under Art 10 TEC (now Art 4 TFEU), to 'take all appropriate measures . . . to ensure the fulfilment of the obligations arising out of this Treaty' and also to 'facilitate the achievement of the Community's tasks'. The Court went on to explain that such obligations also bind all the authorities of the States including, for matters within their jurisdiction, the national courts. Consequently, an obligation is placed on national courts to interpret and apply national law in a manner which is consistent with the wording and purpose of directives.

This judgment has been the subject of much academic criticism as, it is argued, it requires national courts to supplement the role of the domestic legislator. The principle has also been criticised for allowing the direct effect of directives via the 'back door', without the need to ensure that the restrictive *Van Gend* criteria are fulfilled.

The principle has, however, undoubtedly succeeded in enhancing the effectiveness of unimplemented and/or incorrectly implemented directives, while at the same time placing another obstacle in the path of Member States who fail to comply with their obligations.

The development of the doctrine of indirect effect

The *Von Colson* judgment left a number of questions unanswered with regard to the exact extent of the principle of 'indirect effect'.

In Case 80/86, *Kolpinghuis Nijmegen*, the Court made it clear that it would not be possible to interpret national legislation in the light of a directive should this result in conflict with any of the general principles of

Community (now Union) law, such as non-retroactivity or legitimate expectation (Chapter 4 provides consideration of General Principles of EU law). Thus, it is clear that there are limits on the application of indirect effect, and national courts need only interpret national law to conform with directives 'in so far as it is possible'.

In Case C-106/89, *Marleasing*, the Court of Justice confirmed that national legislation, which has been interpreted by a national court in the light of a non-implemented or incorrectly implemented directive, can be relied on, not only by an individual against a State, but also against another individual and even where such national law pre-dates a directive and was not intended to implement it. This would appear to be allowing unincorporated directives to be enforced against individuals, thus achieving 'horizontal direct effect' in all but name. However, the decision in *Marleasing* has been tempered in Case C-456/98, *Centrosteel*, where the European Court provided that a directive cannot of itself impose criminal liability on individuals in the absence of proper implementing legislation. Further, the Court of Justice has confirmed that the interpretive duty only arises once the date for implementation has passed (Case C-212/04, *Adeneler and Others*).

Academics have highlighted that indirect effect is the *most used* means of ensuring proper effect of incorrectly or unimplemented directives and its importance should not, consequently, be underestimated. The Court has regularly reaffirmed its importance and, in joined Cases C-397–403/01 *Pfeiffer and Others* (a case relating to the 'Working Time Directive'), provided that 'the requirement for national law to be interpreted in conformity with Community law is inherent in the system of the Treaty . . . to ensure the full effectiveness of Community law . . .'.

iii. 'Incidental' direct effect

Despite the Court of Justice's decision in *Marshall* (*No 1*) prohibiting the horizontal direct effect of directives, decisions such as in Case C-194/94, *CIA Security International* appear to give horizontal effect to directives, albeit in limited manner. It would seem that where an individual attempts to invoke a directive against another individual *in order to demonstrate the illegality of national legislation* (i.e. where it is being alleged that national law conflicts with the directive) and such illegality is proven, the Court has signalled that EU law (i.e. the directive) must be applied – even where this has some impact on the third party *providing* that no legal obligations are imposed directly on the individual(s) as a result. Once more, the European Court cited the enhanced effectiveness of directives as its aim in allowing this.

In Case C-443/98 *Unilever Italia*, national law was held to be in conflict with an EU directive. The national rule was consequently held to be inapplicable and the directive upheld, which in turn impacted on an individual. However, in this case the Court of Justice explained that 'incidental effect' may only occur where a directive is *not* intended to *directly* confer rights and obligations on individuals – such as a directive introduced in order to protect the internal market, for example. On the other hand, where a directive is introduced with the *aim* of providing individuals with rights and obligations, incidental effect will *not* apply and the 'rule' of no horizontal direct effect of directives will be upheld.

Due to its limitations, it should be noted that the 'incidental effect' of directives is likely to arise only in very limited circumstances.

iv. Additional thoughts on the source of an EU right or obligation

While the matter of the relevant source of a right or obligation (that is, whether the right in question emanates from a treaty article or regulation, for example) is rarely problematic, Case C-144/04, *Mangold* is worth taking a moment to consider. In this case it appeared that the source of the claimant's right was a directive, the expiry date of which had not yet passed. Consequently, the directive could not have direct effect but, as the right in question related to a matter of discrimination, the Court of Justice provided that the right could emanate from the General Principle of Non-discrimination, as opposed to the directive.

It is consequently worth bearing in mind that the source of a right/obligation may not always be as straightforward as it may first appear to be!

5. State liability for damages (The *Francovich* Principle)

In view of the limitations placed on the direct effect of directives, and despite the possibility of enforcing rights under the principle of indirect effect, a number of barriers may still exist with regard to the enforcement of rights emanating from a directive (for example, there may be no national law to interpret or interpretation may simply not be possible due to the wording of the national legislation being very precise).

In Cases C-6 and 9/90, *Francovich and Bonifaci v Italy* (*Francovich*), the Court of Justice held that, should a Member State fail to incorporate a directive into national law, an individual who suffers damage as a consequence may claim compensation from that State, thereby ensuring greater effectiveness of directives.

This right to compensation was, however, subject to a number of criteria, namely:

- the directive must be intended to confer a right on citizens;
- the content of the right must be identifiable by reference to the directive;
- there must be a causal link between the State's breach and the damage suffered.

The Court's judgment in *Francovich* reinforces Member States' obligations under Art 4 TEU and also provides a further incentive to Member States to ensure that EU law rights are not denied to citizens.

i. The development of State damages

The *Francovich* ruling has been of immense importance to Union law and the principle has been clarified and extended in a number of later cases. While in *Francovich*, the Court's decision related to a Member State's failure to fulfil its obligations in relation to directives, in joined Cases C-46 and C-48/93, *Brasserie du Pêcheur SA v Germany; R v Secretary of State for Transport ex p Factortame Ltd and Others* (*Pêcheur and Factortame*), the Court of Justice confirmed that damages could also be available in situations where a Member State had failed to fulfil obligations derived from *other* sources of Union law. Once more, however, the Court explained that certain criteria must be fulfilled:

- the rule of law infringed must be intended to confer rights on individuals;
- the breach must be sufficiently serious;
- there must be a direct causal link between the breach and the damage caused.

The Court also provided that the principle applied to whichever organ of the State was responsible for the breach or omission, whether it be legislative, executive or, controversially, judicial (as in Case C-224/01 *Kobler v Austria*).

ii. The Court of Justice's interpretation of 'sufficiently serious'

With regard to what will constitute a 'sufficiently serious' breach, the Court has put forward various factors that may be taken into account, including the following:

- the degree of clarity and precision of the EU rule that has been breached (if the rule is imprecisely worded, the breach will not be sufficiently serious: Case C-392/93, *R v HM Treasury ex p British Telecom*);

- the 'intentionality' or 'voluntariness' of the infringement and the damage caused (intentional fault is not essential: Cases T-178, 179 and 188–90/94, *Dillenkofer v Germany*);

- the degree of discretion provided to the Member State by the provision (where there is no, or limited, discretion, the infringement of law in itself may be sufficient to establish the existence of a sufficiently serious breach: Case C-5/94, *R v MAFF ex p Hedley Lomas*).

By allowing individuals to bring such actions before their national courts, it should be evident that the Court of Justice has once more enhanced the effectiveness of European Union law. The development of actions for damages against the Member States can be compared with the availability of actions for damages against the Union's Institutions, which have been provided for by the Treaty (Art 340 TFEU, discussed in Chapter 6) and it is quite clear that the Court has been influenced by Art 340 TFEU in regard to the way in which State damages have been developed.

iii. Expansion of the principle to actions against private parties

In addition to the *Francovich* principle being expanded beyond non- or ineffective implementation of directives to any sufficiently serious breach of Union law by a Member State, it would now appear that such actions for damages may also be available against *private* bodies. This can be evidenced by Case C-453-/99, *Courage Ltd v Crehan*. In this case an individual sought to bring an action against another individual for damage suffered as a result of a breach of EU competition law. *As no national remedy was available for the breach*, the Court of Justice confirmed that an action may be brought under the *Francovich* principle, not just against Member States but against private individuals/bodies that cause loss to another through breach of Union law.

II. CONCLUSIONS

Membership of the European Union has resulted in States having an additional source of law to contend with – that of the EU. Perhaps rather surprisingly, the Treaties give little guidance as to the interaction between national and Union law and it has been left to the Court of Justice to interpret which source of law is supreme in situations of conflict and also what effects EU law may have within national legal systems. (It is interesting to note, however, that if the Constitutional Treaty had been given effect, it *would* have contained a statement on the effect of EU law, under what was know as the 'primacy clause'.)

Relatively early in the life of the EEC, the Court of Justice was prepared to explain that Union law is not like other sources of international law. Not only is EU law supreme but it also provides rights and obligations to both States and individuals alike, which can, in turn, be enforced before national courts. The development of principles such as direct effect and supremacy

THE IMPACT OF EUROPEAN UNION LAW:
The Application of Direct Effect

DIRECT EFFECT of Union Law (NOTE: EU law also enjoys SUPREMACY)
What is the source of the EU right?

- **Treaty Article or Regulation:** Enforceable before national court IF source satisfies 3 *Van Gend/Rayners* criteria (if not, right may not be enforceable through direct effect). Capable of vertical and horizontal d/effect (*Defrenne*)

- **Decision:** Enforceable against addressee only IF 3 *Van Gend/Rayners* criteria satisfied (if not, right may not be enforceable)

- **Directive:** More problematic. Enforceable only if 3 *Van Gend/Rayners* criteria are satisfied. Implementation date must have passed (*Ratti*). Only enforceable vertically against a State (*Marshall*). Note the broad interpretation of 'State' (guidance on what may be an emanation of the State provided in *Foster v British Gas*)

ALTERNATIVES TO DIRECT EFFECT: Where Direct Effect is not available, consider:

1. **Indirect Effect (Interpretive Obligation):** National law may be interpreted in light of an unincorporated directive once date for implementation has passed (*Von Volson*) in so far as it is possible to do so (*Marleasing*)

2. **Incidental Direct Effect:** Directive may be given effect where national law and directive conflict and national law is disapplied, thereby giving rights, under the directive, to an individual (*CIA* and *Unilever*). Only available in exceptional circumstances

3. **State Damages:** Available where an individual has suffered loss as a result of MS breach (failure to incorporate directive or other sufficiently serious breach: *Francovich, Pêcheur* and *Factortame*). Criteria must be satisfied

---

have resulted in the Court of Justice being criticised for its 'judicial activism' and for usurping a role that should have been left to the Union's legislators.

While the principles discussed above may appear simplistic and obvious, it should, however, be recognised that their effect on the EU has been profound, elevating its relevance and ensuring its uniform effectiveness throughout the Union.

SOME ISSUES TO THINK ABOUT FURTHER:

- What impact did the Member States originally assume EU law would have on their national legal systems? Which important Court of Justice decision changed this?
- What has been the impact of supremacy and direct effect on the effectiveness of EU law and also on the Union's success in achieving its aims and objectives?
- How has the doctrine of direct effect been developed by the Court of Justice? Why have such developments been considered necessary?

6 Enforcing Union Law

In the preceding chapters, it has been considered why the EEC was created and how it has developed into today's EU, who 'runs' the European Union, the various sources of law that make up the Union's legal system and the relationship between national and EU law. In order to understand how the Union works in practice, we now need to consider how EU law is enforced.

Because EU law forms part of each Member State's domestic legal system, rights and obligations emanating from European law are normally enforced before **domestic courts** rather than before the Court of Justice. This is quite logical – especially if it is remembered that EU law should be viewed as 'just another source' of national law. We therefore need to consider exactly on what basis and how such enforcement takes place.

National courts are not left totally to their own devices when applying EU law and so the procedure known as 'preliminary reference' (Art 267 TFEU), which provides a valuable link between the Court of Justice and domestic courts, will also be considered.

While domestic courts are normally used to enforce EU law rights, there are certain actions that only the Court of Justice has jurisdiction to hear. These include 'infringement proceedings' against Member States who have failed to comply with their EU obligations (Arts 258–260 TFEU) and judicial review of the acts and/or omissions of the Union's institutions (including Arts 263–266 TFEU). Each will be considered in turn.

I. ENFORCING EUROPEAN LAW RIGHTS BEFORE NATIONAL COURTS

As has already been considered in Chapter 5, provided certain criteria are fulfilled, Union law has direct effect, that is, it provides individuals with rights and obligations that are enforceable before national courts. We therefore need to consider which domestic courts may be employed, what procedures should be followed and what remedies should be available to individuals enforcing their EU law rights.

1. Courts

It has been left to the Member States' discretion to decide which national courts will be appropriate to hear actions founded on Union law and also the procedures to be followed. In the United Kingdom, for example, an action relating to EU employment law would be heard before an Employment Tribunal.

As the ECJ stated in Case 45/76, *Comet BV v Produktschap voor Siergewassen* (*Comet*):

> It is for the domestic law of each Member State to designate the courts having jurisdiction and the procedural conditions governing actions at law intended to ensure the protection of the rights which subjects derive from the direct effects of Community law.

2. Procedures

The dicta in *Comet* demonstrate that the enforcement of EU law rights in national courts has to fit in with the national systems already in place for enforcement of national law.

Harmonisation of procedures throughout the EU is not practicable due to the wide variety of approaches employed by the various Member States. Instead, in recognition of the Union's need to ensure the proper enforcement of EU law, while still respecting the autonomy of the Member States, the Court of Justice has laid down guidelines that the national courts are obliged to take into account. These guidelines relate to the following:

- *The principle of non-discrimination*. In the Comet case, the Court provided that its decision was contingent on 'it being understood that such conditions cannot be less favourable than those relating to similar actions of a domestic nature'. This means that although the appropriate court/procedures are left up to the Member States, the States still have an obligation to ensure that national procedures do not discriminate against any individual wishing to enforce an EU law right, as compared to a similar national law right.

- *Availability of an action/remedy*. National procedures must not make it excessively difficult to obtain a remedy for a breach of EU law. In Case 199/82, *Amministrazione delle Finanze dello Stato v San Giorgio (San Giorgio Case)*, the European Court explained that national rules and procedures must not make it, in practice, impossible for rights conferred by the Union to be exercised.

3. Remedies

The Court of Justice has been particularly careful to ensure that appropriate remedies are available with regard to breaches of EU law rules. In Case 33/76, *Rewe-Zentralfinanz v Landschwirtschaftskammer*, the Court explained that although it has been made possible for individuals to bring direct actions based on EU law before national courts, 'it was not intended to create new remedies in the national courts to ensure the observance of Community [now Union] law'.

Consequently, the remedies available for *similar breaches of national law* should be made available for breaches of EU law. However, once more, this has been qualified by guidelines laid down in decisions of the Court of Justice. Again, the provision of a remedy must not discriminate and must be made available 'on the same conditions as would apply were it a question of observing national law' (*Rewe-Zentralfinanz*). In addition, the remedy made available under national law must be an *effective* remedy.

In Case 14/83, *Von Colson*, the Court explained that Art 10 TEC (now largely contained in Art 4 TEC) provides Member States, and therefore their national courts, with the obligation of facilitating the achievement of the aims of the Union. Consequently, Member States and national courts must ensure that remedies available for breaches of EU law must be effective, have a deterrent effect and be 'adequate in relation to the damage sustained' (in other words, be proportionate).

The Court developed this principle in Case 222/84, *Johnston v Chief Constable of the RUC*, emphasising the need to ensure effective judicial protection for those who have suffered as a result of a breach of EU law. It was in Case C-271/91, *Marshall v Southampton and South West Hampshire AHA (Marshall (No 2))* that the European Court took the principle of effectiveness a step further by providing that not only did the remedy have to be comparable with that available for a similar breach of national law but, if no effective remedy was available under national law, national courts should either improve upon what was available or devise a new, suitable remedy. (In *Marshall (No 2)* the UK cap on damages available rendered the remedy ineffective. As a result the UK had to amend its rules.)

i. The development of a uniform Union remedy: State damages

In general, the European Union has been happy to allow national courts to protect the EU law rights of individuals by means of appropriate national procedures and remedies. There has, however, been one exception to this: the development of the Union remedy of 'State damages'.

The development of this remedy has been considered in some detail in Chapter 4. To briefly recap, in Cases C-6 and 9/90, *Francovich*, the Court of Justice provided that, where a Member State had failed to correctly implement the aims of a directive, damages were available from the State to compensate those who had suffered loss as a result of the breach. This ensures that Member States may not rely on, or benefit from, their own wrongdoings and that the remedy for doing so is uniform throughout the European Union.

The remedy is based on the obligations placed on Member States (by what was Art 10 TEC, now Art 4 TEU) and has been developed in later cases (particularly Cases C-46 and 48/93, *Brasserie du Pêcheur* and *Factortame*) to include *any* sufficiently serious breach of EU law by a State or its public bodies or, now also it would seem, private parties *(Crehan* case). A number of criteria must be fulfilled before damages can be made available and these too are considered in Chapter 4, to which you should refer.

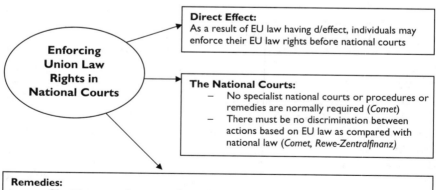

Enforcing Union Law Rights in National Courts

Direct Effect:
As a result of EU law having d/effect, individuals may enforce their EU law rights before national courts

The National Courts:
- No specialist national courts or procedures or remedies are normally required (*Comet*)
- There must be no discrimination between actions based on EU law as compared with national law (*Comet, Rewe-Zentralfinanz*)

Remedies:
- Obtaining a remedy must not be made too difficult (*San Georgio*)
- Remedy must be effective (*Marshall*)
- Remedy will be the same as for breach of national law – exception: State Damages against MS (*Francovich, Pêcheur and Factortame*)

II. PRELIMINARY REFERENCES/ RULINGS

Article 267 TFEU provides the Court of Justice with the jurisdiction to give preliminary rulings on the interpretation of the Treaties and also on the interpretation and validity of acts of the institutions (basically secondary legislation), when requested to do so by national courts.

It should be emphasised at the outset that Art 267 does *not* give the Court authority to decide the outcome of a case but rather to interpret EU law and rule on the validity of EU legislation, other than the Treaties. This can be illustrated in *Arsenal v Reed (No 2)* [2003], where the national court refused to follow a ruling provided by the Court of Justice as they argued that the European Court had exceeded their jurisdiction by making a finding in fact.

Article 267 is often cited as evidence that EU law has always been intended to have direct effect as, if national courts were not intended to enforce EU law, why would they need to make a reference to the Court of Justice at all?

1. The purpose of preliminary rulings

The purpose of Art 267 TFEU is to ensure the **uniform interpretation and application of Union law**. The principle of direct effect has firmly established national courts as enforcers of EU law and if interpretation were left to national courts it would not be possible to ensure uniformity, given that different legal systems employ different interpretative methods. (Consider, for example, the position in the United Kingdom, where the literal method of interpretation is favoured, as opposed to other Member States, who may employ a more purposive approach.)

2. The effects of preliminary rulings

The Court of Justice is not bound by precedent, which means that it does not have to follow its own previous rulings – but in reality it does so in order to ensure consistency (the Court's dicta in Cases 28–30/62, *Da Costa*, in which it repeated its *Van Gend* judgment, are a good example of this).

A referring national court will, however, be bound by the ruling of the Court of Justice and is obliged to apply the ruling obtained to the case before it. While a ruling will normally be retrospective in its effect, the

Court of Justice may limit the temporal effects of any such ruling (as it did in Case C-262/88, *Barber v Guardian Royal Exchange*, where the Court held that the ruling was effective only from the date of its judgment).

Despite national courts being bound by the rulings of the Court of Justice, the Court has, in the past, been at pains to point out that it is not 'senior' to the national courts, but merely has a different function to perform. In reality, however, the European Court undoubtedly enjoys a superior position.

3. Which national bodies may make a reference?

Article 267 TFEU provides that 'any court or tribunal of a Member State' may make a reference. The European Court has accepted references from a variety of national courts and tribunals, including arbitration panels, insurance officers and administrative tribunals (the reference in *Van Gend* came from a Dutch Administrative Tribunal). Consideration of case law demonstrates, however, that the Court of Justice does not have the jurisdiction to accept a reference from a body that lies outside the legal system of a Member State. In Case 102/81, *Nordsee*, for example, a request for a ruling was made by an arbitration tribunal that had been established by contract – the reference was consequently refused. Conversely, in Case 246/80, *Broekmeulen*, the Court considered that a Dutch body known as the Appeals Committee for General Medicine was an appropriate body as it operated with the consent and co-operation of the public authorities and delivered decisions which were recognised as final in law.

4. The decision to refer

A national court or tribunal will only need to make a reference where it considers that its decision in the case before it rests on a point of EU law. Article 267 TFEU makes it clear that it is for the national court to decide when a reference should be made and *not* the parties to a case or any other party or authority, including the Court of Justice. (National precedent should never operate to prevent a court from seeking a ruling, as evidenced by Cases 146 and 166/73, *Rheinmühlen-Düsseldorf.*) The Treaty also distinguishes between those national courts that have the *discretion* to refer and those that are *obliged* to refer.

i. The discretion to refer

Article 267(2) TFEU provides that any court 'may, if it considers that a decision on the question is necessary to enable it to give judgment, request the Court of Justice to give a ruling thereon'. The Court of Justice has interpreted this to mean that where an appropriate body is called upon to reach a decision which may based on an issue of EU law, that body has the authority to make a reference to the European Court (Case 92/78, *Simmenthal*) but is not bound to do so.

ii. The obligation to refer

Article 267(3) TFEU provides that national courts or tribunals 'against whose decisions there is no judicial remedy in national law . . . **shall** bring the matter before the Court of Justice'. Thus, any court from which there is no appeal *must* make a reference when called upon to reach a decision on a matter that relates to a point of Union law. There have been conflicting opinions, however, as to which national courts this obligation applies to.

Under what became known as the 'abstract theory', it was argued that only courts from which no appeal was available would be obliged to refer. (In the UK, for example, Lord Denning in *Bulmer v Bollinger* (1974) considered that only the House of Lords [now the Supreme Court] fell into this category.) However, under the opposing 'concrete theory' it was thought that where the parties had no *automatic right* of appeal, the national court was obliged to refer. This theory was considered the most persuasive, as it was supported by the Court of Justice in cases such as *Costa v ENEL*.

Following the Swedish Case 99/00, *Lyckeskog*, the position appears to have changed once more. In this case an appeal from a Swedish district court could only be made with the agreement of the Swedish Supreme Court. The Court of Justice provided that as there was a *possibility* of an appeal (even though leave to appeal may be refused) the district court was not to be considered the court of last resort. Thus it would appear that the 'abstract theory' is now the favoured approach.

iii. Acte clair

Despite the obligation to refer provided by Art 267(3) TFEU, it should be noted that there are *three* circumstances in which the Court of Justice has specifically held that it may *not* be necessary for a national court to make a reference, even if circumstances suggest that the 'abstract theory' applies. This has become known as *'acte clair'* (borrowed from French law). The circumstances in which *acte clair* applies were explained by the Court in Case 283/81, *CILFIT*, and are as follows:

- the question of EU law is irrelevant to the case being heard by the national court;
- the question of EU law has already been interpreted by the Court of Justice in a previous ruling. (This principle was first established in the *Da Costa* case. As the Court of Justice does not have to follow its own previous rulings, national courts should, however, recognise the possibility that the Court may amend its original ruling and bear this in mind when taking their decision as to whether to refer or not);
- the correct interpretation is *so obvious* as to leave no scope for reasonable doubt. (This rule has been criticised, as what may be 'obvious' to one national court may not be so obvious to another, leaving room for lack of uniformity.)

It should be noted that the Court of Justice has not *precluded* national courts from making a reference in the above circumstances; it has merely removed the obligation. In addition, the Court has explained that where a national court *is* under an obligation to refer (i.e. none of the above 'exceptions' apply) but does *not*, the State may be liable in damages (under the principle of *Francovich* – or State – damages, Chapter 5) for the failure of that court (Case C-224/01, *Kobler v Austria*).

5. Can the Court of Justice refuse to provide a ruling?

As already considered, the decision to refer is the national courts' alone and may not be questioned by the Court of Justice. The European Court has, however, on occasion, declined to give a ruling.

We have already considered instances where the Court has refused a ruling due to the fact that the national body making the ruling lay outside the Member State's legal system. In addition, in Cases 104/79 and 244/80, *Foglia v Novello* (*Nos 1 and 2*), the Court of Justice concluded that it had no jurisdiction to provide a ruling in a dispute which had been 'fabricated' by the parties, as their role was not to give abstract or advisory opinions. In Case C-83/91, *Meilicke*, the Court similarly concluded that it would exceed its jurisdiction if it answered hypothetical questions.

It has also withheld its opinion where proceedings have terminated in the national court (Case 338/85, *Pardini*) and also when it has felt that it has been given insufficient information or the question was too vague (the Court has issued guidance on this matter in 'Guidance on references by national courts for preliminary rulings' [1997] 1 CMLR 78).

From examination of the above and other case law, it can be concluded that the Court of Justice may refuse to provide a ruling, but only in circumstances where to provide such a ruling would amount to an abuse of the preliminary reference procedure.

6. The referral procedure

Where a national court reaches the conclusion that a reference is appropriate, it must formulate a question or questions to refer to the Court of Justice. (Where such questions are in some way inappropriate, the European Court has, in the past, shown itself willing to reformulate them in a manner that will best assist the national court, although there is growing evidence that the Court has become less willing to do this due, perhaps, to pressure of work.) The national court will also need to provide issues of fact and national law relevant to the case in question. The national court must stay proceedings until the ruling of the Court of Justice is transmitted back to it.

Being of general interest, once the Court has received a reference, it will be translated into all official languages of the Union, notified to the Member States and EU Institutions and noted in the Official Journal. Written observations will be accepted from the parties, Member States and Institutions, and there will be a brief opportunity for oral submissions to be put before the Court (these will be in the official language of the national court that referred the question). The Court of Justice will deliberate the matter, after receiving the opinion of the Advocate General (AG), finally providing a judgment which will be reached by majority vote. This decision will then not only be returned to the national court, but also published.

It is important to remember that, while the Court of Justice has jurisdiction to pronounce on the validity of EU secondary legislation and interpret the Treaties, it is not the function of the Court to decide the outcome of the case before the national court. The national court must perform this function.

7. The consequences of the preliminary reference procedure

The availability of preliminary references has had a number of important consequences.

First, it has forged a link between national legal systems and the EU's legal system. Without such rulings, national courts and the Court of Justice would remain isolated from one another. Second, the availability of a reference affords national courts the opportunity to familiarise themselves with the European Union's legal order.

Of particular importance is the manner in which the Court has used the process in order to develop the EU's legal system and constitutionalise the Treaties. The Court has clarified the extent of EU law through its development of principles such as direct effect and supremacy in seminal judgments such as *Van Gend* and *Costa* (discussed in Chapter 5). In addition, preliminary references have been the vehicle by which General Principles of EU law have been articulated (discussed in Chapter 4).

In conjunction with Art 10 TEC (now incorporated by Art 4 TEU), the Court has also been able to further extend the scope and effectiveness of the EU's legal order, developing such principles as the 'interpretative obligation' (*Von Colson*) and 'State damages' (*Francovich*). Further protection has been afforded to individuals by the Court, which has ensured, for

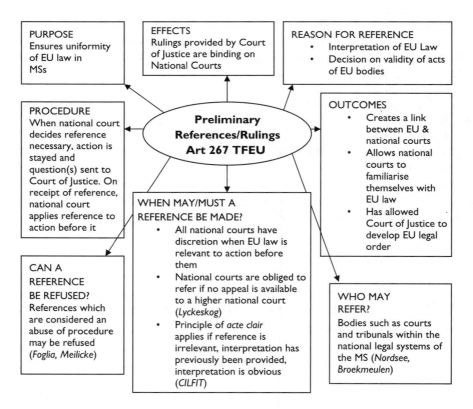

The Preliminary Reference Procedure

example, that the remedies available for breach of EU law rights are effective (as in *Marshall (No 2)*) and available to as many citizens as possible (such as in *Hoekstra*, discussed further in Chapter 8).

Finally, it should be noted that the process can afford individuals with an alternative opportunity to challenge the validity of acts of the Institutions, an issue which is discussed further, below.

III. ENFORCEMENT ACTIONS AGAINST MEMBER STATES (ARTS 258–260 TFEU)

Member States have a duty to fulfil the obligations placed on them by EU law (for example, Art 4 TEU provides a general duty, while numerous Treaty articles provide specific obligations). It is therefore necessary to consider how EU law ensures that all Member States comply with these obligations.

1. Actions brought by the Commission (Art 258 TFEU)

Should a Member State breach EU law and an individual suffer as a result, that individual may of course bring an action against an errant State (under the doctrine of direct effect, discussed in Chapter 5). The TFEU, however, provides other methods of ensuring that States comply with their obligations.

Article 258 TFEU gives the Commission the authority to investigate and, if necessary, bring before the Court of Justice any Member State which it considers may have failed to fulfil its EU obligations. The Commission's powers are, however, discretionary and the Commission cannot be *forced* to act against a State (Case 48/65, *Lutticke*), although a refusal may be the subject of a complaint to the European Ombudsman (Art 228 TFEU).

It is perfectly possible for an individual to bring a direct action against a State while, at the same time, the Commission is also initiating enforcement proceedings. This can be evidenced by the *Factortame* series of cases, together with Case C-246/89R, *Commission v UK*. Both acts and omissions of the Member States are open to scrutiny (Case 167/73, *Commission v France*).

Investigations under Art 258 TFEU are initiated by the Commission, either on its own initiative or following a complaint. (It should be noted that the complainant does not play any further role in the proceedings, as they are not intended as a means by which individuals can obtain redress.) Actions may be divided into two stages – the administrative stage and the judicial stage. The administrative stage can be further subdivided into the informal and the formal.

i. The Commission's investigative powers

Where the Commission suspects a Member State is in breach of its EU obligations, the Commission will enter into (informal) dialogue with the appropriate authorities within that State. This stage is very important, as the majority of alleged breaches are resolved without the need for further intervention by the Commission. (It would appear that many States fail to comply with their obligations due to ignorance or misunderstanding and, in such circumstances, they are normally quick to remedy their breach.)

If the alleged breach is not rectified at this stage, the Commission may issue a formal letter, defining the breach and requesting that the Member State submit its observations within a reasonable amount of time (normally two months). If the issue remains unresolved at the end of this period, the Commission will deliver a 'reasoned opinion', setting out how the Member State has violated its EU law obligations and allowing it a reasonable time (again usually two months, but this will depend on individual circumstances) to remedy the alleged breach. The reasoned opinion is very important in that it establishes the scope of the action and the legal arguments on which the Commission is relying.

ii. Judicial proceedings

If the breach is not remedied by the Member State within the time stated in the reasoned opinion, the Commission will proceed to the judicial stage, referring the matter to the Court of Justice. Even at this stage, it may be possible to settle the action before the Court gives judgment. Where judgment is given, only about one in ten decisions favour the Member State. This is not surprising, as the Commission is unlikely to proceed if its case is weak. In addition, the Court has shown itself unreceptive to the majority of defences argued by Member States.

In Case 128/78, *Commission v UK* (the *Tachograph* case), for example, the UK argued 'practical difficulties' due to trade union resistance to the introduction of tachographs in the cabs of lorries, while in Cases 227–30/85, *Commission v Belgium*, it was argued that failure of regional, rather than central, government had caused the breach. The Court accepted neither argument. In Case 101/84, *Commission v Italy*, Italy did not submit statistics required by Europe as a bomb attack on a data processing centre had destroyed relevant data. Italy argued *force majeure*, which was again not accepted by the Court.

iii. Non-compliance with the Court's judgment

If the European Court finds that a Member State is in breach of its EU obligations, it will issue a declaration to that effect, requiring that the breach be *immediately* remedied. Until amendments made by the Maastricht Treaty were introduced, such judgments of the Court were of declaratory effect only, the only remedy for failure to comply being the possibility of further enforcement proceedings being initiated by the Commission, again under Art 258 TFEU.

Now under Art 260 TFEU, the Commission may, after giving the State an opportunity to submit its observations, once more refer the case to the Court, this time specifying an appropriate pecuniary penalty (fine) to be levied against the errant Member State. If the Court again finds against the State, it may levy a fine, not exceeding that specified by the Commission.

This has had the effect of providing an originally rather toothless action with the necessary teeth, although it is not yet clear what the outcome would be if a Member State refused to pay any fine imposed. This question has been the topic of academic debate, with a favoured suggestion being the removal of a defaulting Member State's voting rights.

2. Actions brought by Member States

If one Member State considers that another Member State has failed to fulfil its Community obligations, then the first State may bring the matter before the Court of Justice under Art 259 TFEU, but the procedure first requires that the matter be brought to the attention of the Commission. Proceedings then mirror those set out under Art 258 TFEU, other than the requirement that the Commission request the observations of *both* Member States concerned.

In addition, the Commission is required to deliver a reasoned opinion within three months of the matter being brought to its attention. If the Commission fails to provide a reasoned opinion within this time, the complainant Member State may bring the matter before the Court. Should the Court find a violation, matters proceed as already set out above.

Actions brought under Art 259 TFEU are extremely rare. This is understandable, as Member States prefer to make an informal complaint to the Commission rather than choose the far more politically contentious Art 259 TFEU route.

3. The effectiveness of enforcement procedures

Although no official figures are available on the success of the informal investigative stage followed by the Commission, the administrative stage as a whole has proven itself particularly successful in resolving breaches, and the vast majority of breaches are resolved without the need to refer the matter to the Court of Justice. (Statistics can be found in the Commission's Annual Report, available from the Europa website.) This suggests that the

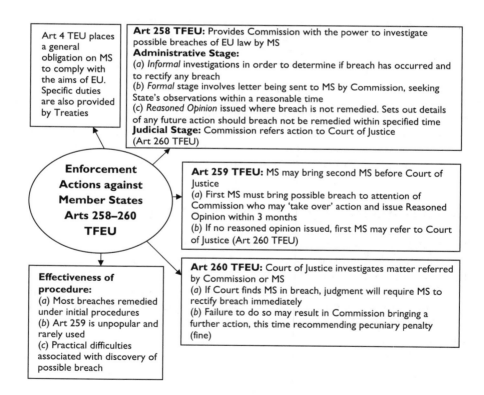

Art 4 TEU places a general obligation on MS to comply with the aims of EU. Specific duties are also provided by Treaties

Art 258 TFEU: Provides Commission with the power to investigate possible breaches of EU law by MS
Administrative Stage:
(a) *Informal* investigations in order to determine if breach has occurred and to rectify any breach
(b) *Formal* stage involves letter being sent to MS by Commission, seeking State's observations within a reasonable time
(c) *Reasoned Opinion* issued where breach is not remedied. Sets out details of any future action should breach not be remedied within specified time
Judicial Stage: Commission refers action to Court of Justice (Art 260 TFEU)

Enforcement Actions against Member States Arts 258–260 TFEU

Art 259 TFEU: MS may bring second MS before Court of Justice
(a) First MS must bring possible breach to attention of Commission who may 'take over' action and issue Reasoned Opinion within 3 months
(b) If no reasoned opinion issued, first MS may refer to Court of Justice (Art 260 TFEU)

Effectiveness of procedure:
(a) Most breaches remedied under initial procedures
(b) Art 259 is unpopular and rarely used
(c) Practical difficulties associated with discovery of possible breach

Art 260 TFEU: Court of Justice investigates matter referred by Commission or MS
(a) If Court finds MS in breach, judgment will require MS to rectify breach immediately
(b) Failure to do so may result in Commission bringing a further action, this time recommending pecuniary penalty (fine)

Enforcement Actions against the Member States

administrative stage of enforcement procedures is particularly successful, in that it allows the Commission to 'educate' Member States and ensure that they are aware of their EU obligations.

However, also important with regard to the effectiveness of enforcement actions is the Commission's ability – or lack of it – to uncover possible breaches. The Commission has no 'police force' that it can enlist to assist in the uncovering of breaches by the Member States and it is likely that very many continue unnoticed. In recognition of this, the Commission has employed technology to encourage citizens and companies to notify them of possible breaches on their website.

The Commission has also recognised that breaches will often be the result of a Member State's failure to implement directives. The Commission has sought to remedy this by requiring that directives be published in the Official Journal and also by insisting that Member States notify them when directives are incorporated into national law.

It can be concluded that enforcement procedures, particularly the administrative stage of Art 258 TFEU, play an important role in ensuring that Union aims are achieved and Union law is upheld.

IV. ACTIONS AGAINST EU INSTITUTIONS: JUDICIAL REVIEW OF THE ACTS AND OMISSIONS OF UNION BODIES

The Treaties provide the Union's institutions with a number of powers and obligations. As in all developed legal systems, a mechanism has been put into place through which the manner in which these obligations are discharged can be reviewed.

Judicial review is the term commonly used to describe a variety of causes of action relating to the review of acts or decisions of the Union's Institutions. It includes annulment actions (Art 263 TFEU) and actions for failure to act (Art 265 TFEU). 'Judicial review' also covers applications for interim measures relating to other judicial procedures (Art 279 TFEU). These procedures are part of the system of 'checks and balances' which exist to ensure that the Union bodies act within the limits of the powers afforded them by the Treaties.

1. Judicial review: action to annul (Arts 263 and 264 TFEU)

Article 263 TFEU is the primary method by which the legality of the acts of the Union's institutions may be challenged. If such a challenge is successful, the act will be declared void by the Court of Justice (Art 264 TFEU). Basically, this action allows the validity of rules enacted by the Institutions and other Union bodies to be challenged.

i. Whose acts may be challenged?

Article 263 TFEU provides the Court of Justice with the jurisdiction to review the 'legality of legislative acts of the Council, the Commission and the European Central Bank and of the European Parliament and European Council, where such acts are intended to produce legal effects vis à vis third parties, it shall also review the acts of bodies, offices and agencies of the Union intended to produce legal effects vis à vis third parties'. Prior to amendments introduced by the Maastricht Treaty, the TEC only referred to acts adopted by the Council and the Commission. The Court of Justice had, however, already declared the acts of the European Parliament (EP) to be reviewable prior to such amendments (Case 294/83, *Parti Ecologiste 'Les Verts' v European Parliament*).

ii. What acts may be challenged?

Consideration of the wording of Art 263 TFEU reveals that legislative acts 'other than recommendations and opinions' (neither of which have any binding force: Art 288 TFEU) may be challenged and also acts which 'produce legal effects vis à vis third parties'. As a result the Court has interpreted the Article broadly to include any act which is **capable of having legal effects** as challengeable (Case 22/70, *Commission v Council*, the ERTA case).

However, since the enactment of the Treaty of Lisbon, Art 263(4) TFEU has been amended to include 'regulatory acts', a term which is not defined by the Treaty. Such acts were, however, explained by the defunct Constitutional Treaty, which described them as 'non-legislative' acts. It has been suggested that such acts should be thought of as acts used to *implement* EU law or 'quasi-judicial' acts of an administrative nature, thus broadening those acts which are challengeable. However, at the time of writing, the Court has yet to interpret the term and consequently this is something which students should be alert to!

iii. Grounds for bringing a challenge

The Treaty lists the following grounds under which an action may be brought:

- *lack of competence* – this occurs where the Union bodies act in areas where they are not authorised to do so by the Treaties;
- *infringement of an essential procedural requirement* – for example, the Council failing to consult the EP (Case 138/79, *Roquette Frères v Council*);
- *infringement of the Treaties or any rule of law relating to its application* – this ground often overlaps with others. The Court has explained that it can include a breach of one of the general principles of Union law (Case 4/73, *Nold v Commission*);
- *misuse of powers* – this ground will be relevant where an institution has used its power(s) for a purpose other than that for which they were intended.

iv. Who can bring an action?

This has proved to be a controversial area and is, consequently, often the subject of examination questions! Applicants can be divided into those with automatic *locus standi* (see Glossary), that is 'privileged applicants', and those who have to prove an interest, that is 'semi-privileged' and 'non-privileged' applicants, each of which will be considered in turn:

Privileged applicants

Article 263 TFEU gives automatic *locus standi* to Member States, the European Parliament, the Council and the Commission. (The position of the EP as a litigant was again amended by the Maastricht Treaty. While the Court had already accepted the Parliament's right to bring an action in Case C-70/88, *European Parliament v Council* (the *Chernobyl* case), it was not until the TEU came into force that this was formalised.)

Semi-privileged applicants

In cases where their prerogatives (rights or interests) are affected, Art 263 TFEU provides that the Court of Auditors, the ECB and the Committee of Regions may commence an action.

Non-privileged applicants

Article 263 TFEU provides that any natural or legal person (in effect an individual or business) may bring an action in three circumstances:

(a) where the applicant is the *addressee* of an act;

(b) where an act is of *'direct and individual concern'* to the applicant;

(c) where there is a *'regulatory act'*, which is of direct concern to the applicant, not entailing implementing measures.

Where the applicant is the addressee of an act
Where an applicant can demonstrate that s/he is the *addressee* of an act – such as a decision (consult Art 288 TFEU) – they will have little problem demonstrating *locus standi*.

Where an applicant has to demonstrate 'direct and individual concern'
Where an act has not been addressed to the applicant, the Article also provides *locus standi* where an act is of *'direct and individual concern'* to that applicant. It therefore needs to be considered how 'direct and individual concern' has been interpreted by the Court.

The Court of Justice developed a 'test' to ascertain **individual concern** in Case 25/62, *Plaumann v Commission*, often referred to as the *'Plaumann* Formula'. In that case, the applicant was a clementine importer. He sought to challenge a decision addressed to the German Government, as it allowed Germany to amend the duty on clementines imported from outside the EU. The Court of Justice prescribed that, in order to demonstrate 'individual concern', the applicant must be able to show that he was *distinguishable from other persons generally*, due to certain attributes or circumstances: in other words, he had to show he was a member of a 'closed class'. In addition, he was required to demonstrate that, by virtue of those attributes or circumstances, he should be singled out in the same way as the addressee of the Directive.

Plaumann failed in his action because, as the Court pointed out, any other person could, if they so wished, carry out the commercial activity in which he was involved and he was consequently not held to be part of a 'closed class'. The test has been confirmed in a number of cases and, for example, those who have entered into a contract (Case 11/82, *Piraiki-Patraiki v Commission)* and those who have applied for a licence (Cases 106 & 107/63, *Toepfer v Commisson)* have been held to come within the necessary 'closed class'. (It should be understood that an applicant does not have to be part of a class of one to be seen as in a 'closed class'.)

This test remains the seminal case in this area, despite being criticised as unduly restrictive and also despite being the subject of much judicial activity. In March 2002, AG Jacobs delivered an Opinion in Case C-50/00P, *Union de Pequeños Agricultores v Council* (the *UPA* case), in which he proposed that there be a redefinition of the test for 'individual concern'. A short time later, the Court of First Instance appeared to support this approach in Case

T-177/01, *Jégo Quéré v Commission*, also suggesting that the rather narrow definition provided in *Plaumann* be broadened and made easier to satisfy. The Court of Justice, however, rejected the positions of both the AG and the CFI, arguing that it was not for them to reform the conditions for *locus standi* but that it should be a matter for legislation. It was argued that this was rather a surprising stance for the Court of Justice to take, given its previous willingness in *other* areas to ensure citizens have sufficient opportunity to enforce their rights. It has also been pointed out that there is nothing in the wording of what was then Art 230 TEC to suggest that such a restrictive interpretation be provided.

It is also relevant to note that where the legislative act in question was a regulation, individual concern could not be proven as regulations have general application (Art 288 TFEU) and cannot therefore only apply to a 'closed class'. The Court, however, took a broader approach, explaining that it would look behind the form of the act to the substance in order to determine its true nature (e.g. Cases 41–44/70, *International Fruit Co v Commission*) thus allowing, in prescribed circumstances, that a regulation could be challenged.

This ensures that the institutions cannot reduce the opportunity for challenge by choosing a legislative form that is not open to question by individuals. The same 'closed category' test as in *Plaumann* will be applied to demonstrate 'individual concern'. (Case C-309/89, *Cordoniu v Council*, and in Cases 789 and 790/79, *Calpak*.)

Where an applicant succeeds in demonstrating 'individual concern', he must also prove that the act was of '**direct concern**' to him. According to the Court of Justice's interpretation, this requires that the applicant show that (a) the act has directly affected his legal position, and (b) a direct link exists between the act complained of and the loss/damage suffered, which can be compared to demonstrating 'causation' under English and Welsh law. (An illustrative case is *International Fruit Co v Commission*.)

The Court has also added that the measure can only be of direct concern where no discretion is afforded to the Member State(s) with regard to its implementation (in Cases 10 and 18/68, *Eridania v Commission*, for example, a Commission Decision relating to the provision of aid was considered not to be of direct concern as authority relating to the allocation of such aid was given to the State).

Where a regulatory act is being challenged
As has already been touched upon above, since the enactment of the Treaty of Lisbon, Art 263(4) TFEU has been amended to include '*regulatory acts*', a term which is not defined by the Treaty. However, such acts were described in the now-defunct Constitutional Treaty as measures of a non-legislative

nature, enacted to implement EU law. At the time of writing, the Court of Justice has yet to provide an interpretation of 'regulatory act' and this is something to which you should keep alert.

Where an act can be seen to be a 'regulatory act', the applicant will only be required to demonstrate direct concern.

v. Time limits

The Treaty imposes a time limit of two months on the bringing of an action. This time starts to run either from the publication of the measure, from its notification to the claimant, or from the day on which it came, or should have come, to the attention of the claimant.

vi. Effects of annulment

Article 264 TFEU provides that if the Court finds an application for annulment well founded, the act should be declared void. Normally, nullity will be considered to be retroactive, although the Court has shown itself willing to limit the temporal effects in appropriate circumstances, particularly where an innocent party may otherwise suffer loss (Case 81/72, *Commission v Council*).

Under Art 266 TFEU, the Institutions are obliged to act to comply with the judgment of the Court. The Treaty does not provide any sanction should an institution fail to comply with a judgment (unlike the position where a Member State fails to comply), although by failing to comply, an Institution may find itself vulnerable to claims for damages under Art 340 TFEU, which is discussed in further detail below.

2. Judicial review: actions for failure to Act (Arts 265 and 266 TFEU)

Actions under Art 265 TFEU can be seen as the other side of the coin from actions under Art 263 TFEU. While the latter renders acts of the Institutions ineffective, the former may be used to compel an institution to fulfil its EU obligations. An action will consequently only be available where the applicant can show that such an obligation exists.

i. Whose failure to act can be challenged?

Article 265 TFEU provides that 'Should the European Parliament, the European Council, the Council, the Commission or the European Central

Bank, in infringement of the Treaties, fail to act . . .' making it clear which of the Union's institutions may be challenged. The Treaty also provides that 'This article shall apply . . . to bodies and agencies of the Union which fail to act', extending the scope of the Article.

ii. Who may make a challenge?

The Treaty provides the Member States and all Institutions with automatic *locus standi*. Natural and legal persons once more have limited *locus standi* and may only bring an action where an institution has an obligation to address an act (other than an opinion or a recommendation) to him, her or it. The applicant must demonstrate direct and individual concern and the Court will apply the same restrictive tests as have been established for Art 263 TFEU (Case C-107/91, *ENU v Commission*).

iii. Procedure in Art 265 TFEU

Actions will only be admissible where the institution or body has first been called upon to act by the challenger, thus providing the institution concerned with the opportunity to remedy its alleged omission.

Once a request for action has been made, the institution or body must then define its position within two months of being called upon to act. Once an institution has defined its position, no further action is possible – even where the institution fails to act (Case 48/65, *Alfons Lutticke v Commission*). If the institution does *not* define its position, any action is then subject to a time limit of a further two months.

Given that an institution or body need only define its position in order to avoid an action, it is not surprising that there have not been many successful actions under Art 265!

iv. Consequences of a successful action

Article 266 TFEU provides that institutions are obliged to comply with the Court's ruling under Art 265 TFEU.

3. Actions which may provide an alternative to judicial review/actions to annul

It is obvious that bringing an action under either Art 263 or 265 TFEU can present particular problems for individuals, both natural and legal, due to the difficulties associated with proving *locus standi*. In addition, neither

Article provides the opportunity for claiming damages. It is therefore important to consider possible alternatives.

Such actions are considered, albeit briefly, below.

i. Preliminary references

As has already been considered above, the preliminary reference procedure (Art 267 TFEU) allows national courts to put questions relating to the validity of Union acts before the Court of Justice. While preliminary references do *not* provide individuals with a direct action, they may nevertheless provide a channel through which an indirect challenge may be mounted.

For example, where the time limit cannot be satisfied or where an individual has not been able to demonstrate the necessary *locus standi* to bring an action to annul (judicial review) under Art 263 TFEU, it may be possible to challenge an act through the preliminary reference procedure. This will only be possible, however, where there is a separate action before the national court – perhaps where the applicant has been brought before the court due to his/her alleged failure to comply with the act in question: it is not possible to bring such an action on the basis of a request for a preliminary reference. In addition, it should be remembered that while an applicant may ask the national court to make a reference, they cannot demand that such a reference be made.

The Court of Justice has, however, made it clear that the *primary* method of challenge is that under Art 263 TFEU and that a challenge brought under Art 267 (Preliminary Reference) will only be available where judicial review is *not* an option open to a claimant. This was highlighted in Case C-188/92, TWD *Textilwerke Deggendorf*, where the Court held that to request a ruling under Art 267 was an abuse of procedure. In this case the applicant chose not to challenge a Commission Decision under Art 230 TEC (now Art 263 TFEU) within the two-month time limit.

ii. Plea of illegality (Art 277 TFEU)

Article 227 TFEU provides a means of indirect challenge against 'an act of general application adopted by an institution, body or agency of the Union'. An example of such an act would be a regulation and, until the coming into force of the Treaty of Lisbon, the Article only referred to regulations, although the Court demonstrated flexibility by showing itself willing to look at the substance rather than just the form of an act (Case 92/78, *Simmenthal*).

A plea of illegality is not, however, an independent action (Cases 31 and 33/62, *Wohrmann and Lutticke v Commission*). It is only available as a defence, where other proceedings have been brought against the applicant, and the Court of Justice has explained that the purpose of the action is to allow individuals' protection from the application of an illegal regulation. The action may be pleaded on the same grounds as those found under Art 263 TFEU.

The effect of a successful challenge is that the act will be declared inapplicable in that case, but it will not be declared void. Any measures based on the act will, however, be automatically void and subsequent measures based on the act will also be open to challenge.

4. Actions for damages (Art 340 TFEU)

i. Contractual liability

Article 340(1) TFEU provides that the 'contractual liability of the Union shall be governed by the law applicable to the contract in question'. When an individual wishes to make a claim against a Union institution for damages in relation to a contractual matter, the action must therefore be brought in the appropriate *national* court and under the legal rules appropriate to the Member State in which the contract is enforceable.

ii. Non-contractual liability

Article 340(2) TFEU relates to the EU's non-contractual liability. Under the jurisdiction afforded to it by Art 268 TFEU, the Court of Justice may hear actions brought against the Union in relation to damage caused either by its:

- Institutions, including the European Central Bank (*fautes de service*), or
- servants (*fautes personnelles*), in the performance of their duties (the concept of vicarious liability is relevant here but has limitations, as is illustrated in Case 9/69, *Sayag v Leduc*, which is worth reading).

The liability of the Union is to be 'in accordance with the general principles common to the laws of the Member States' and consequently the Court of Justice has looked to the laws of the Member States for guidance on the application of the Article.

Locus standi and time limits

Actions brought under Art 340(2) are independent actions and as such there are no limitations on who may bring a claim: in other words, *locus standi* does not need to be demonstrated (Case 48/65, *Lutticke*). However, a time limit of five years from the time of 'injury', or from the time when the claimant should have reasonably known of it, is imposed.

Breaches may either be administrative *or* legislative in nature.

Liability for administrative acts

Where an action is brought in relation to the manner in which Union rules have been applied or the manner in which staff have carried out their duties, the EU may be liable for both wrongful acts and omissions.

Liability may, for example, involve negligence (Case 14/60, *Meroni*) or failure to consider relevant facts, to accord individuals certain procedural rights or to adequately supervise bodies to whom power has been delegated. The relative seriousness of the 'error' may also be taken into account (Case 145/83, *Adams v Commission* is a helpful case to which you may want to refer).

Liability for legislative acts

At one time, liability in terms of legislative acts was divided into two distinct types by the Court of Justice: liability involving 'economic policy choices' and liability involving 'other' acts.

Breaches involving economic policy choices were governed by a test known as the *'Schoppenstedt* formula' following the Court's dicta in Case 5/71, *Schoppenstedt v Commission*. However, since the Court's decision in Case C-352/98P, *Bergaderm, a* single test covering both types of breach would now appear to be in favour.

The conditions for liability

In order to succeed in an action for damages, three matters must be considered:

- Was the EU rule which is alleged to have been breached **intended to confer rights on individuals**? This may include not only rights contained in legislation but also in the general principles of Union law (*Schoppenstedt*).

- Was the breach **sufficiently serious**? Issues such as the complexity of situations and difficulties in application of interpretation should be taken into account. At the heart of the modern test, however, lies the issue of discretion. Basically, where there is little or no discretion, then all that may be necessary is for the claimant to prove sufficiently serious breach on the part of the institution. However, where the institution has been provided with some degree of discretion, some degree of 'blameworthiness' must be demonstrated (Case T-351/03 *Schneider v Commission*).

- Is there a **causal link** between the breach and the damage complained of? The amount claimed must be actual, certain and concrete (Case 26/74, *Société Roquette Frères v Commission*). With regard to causation, the Court has made it clear that the applicant must demonstrate two things: the act caused the loss/damage and the chain of causation has not been broken. The chain of causation may be broken by the actions of a Member State, in which case it will be the State, as opposed to the EU, that will be liable, unless the EU has failed to adequately exercise its supervisory power over the State (*Lutticke*). If there is joint liability on the part of the Union and a Member State, the Member State will generally be considered to be primarily liable and the action should

---

PURPOSE OF JUDICIAL REVIEW:

Part of the 'checks and balances' which ensure that EU bodies act within the powers afforded them by EU law

Judicial Review: Actions to Challenge the Acts of the Institutions

ALTERNATIVE CHALLENGES:

(a) Validity of acts of EU bodies may be challenged under the Preliminary Reference procedure BUT consider difficulties

(b) Plea of Illegality (Art 277 TFEU). May only be used as a defence

(c) Failure to act where there is a duty may be challenged under Art 265 TFEU

(d) Action for damages (Art 340 TFEU) in regard to contractual liability OR loss caused by an institution or its staff

ACTION TO ANNUL: Arts 263 & 264 TFEU

(a) *Who has jurisdiction to hear a challenge?*
Court of Justice of the EU

(b) *Whose acts may be challenged?*
Council, Commission, EP, EC and ECB

(c) *What acts may be challenged?*
Any act capable of legal effects (*ERTA* Case)

(d) *On what grounds may a challenge be brought?*
Lack of competence, infringement of a procedural requirement, infringement of law, misuse of power

(e) *Who may bring a challenge?* Those with *locus standi*, namely:
  – Privileged applicants: MSs, EP, Council, Commission
  – Semi-privileged applicants: CoA, ECB & Committee of Regions
  – Non-privileged applicants: the most problematic group. Legal persons who are the addressee of an act OR where applicant can prove **direct** (*International Fruit* Case) AND **individual** concern (*Plaumann* Case) OR, in the case of a 'regulatory act', direct concern

(f) *Time limits:*
Normally within 2 months of publication

(g) *Outcome of a successful challenge:*
Act will be declared void (Art 264 TFEU)

Challenging the Acts of the EU Institutions

then be brought in the appropriate national court. Contributory negligence may also serve to defeat a claim or at least reduce the quantum of damages (*Adams*).

It will be evident from the above discussion that liability for damage caused to individuals by a legislative act of one or more of the Union institutions, or their staff, bears a strong resemblance to liability under the principle of **State liability in damages** available against the Member States (discussed in Chapter 5). In Cases C 46–48/94, *Brasserie du Pecheur*, the Court of Justice made this very clear by providing that the test for State liability and non-contractual damage should not differ.

Finally, it should be remembered that an action for damages may be brought independently *or* in addition to any claim under **Arts 263 and 265 TFEU**.

V. CONCLUSIONS

Union law places rights and obligations on individuals, Member States and EU institutions alike. European law would, however, have little effect if such rights and obligations were unenforceable, and so the Union's legal system includes a variety of means by which it can be ensured that all comply with European law.

When an individual (natural or artificial) breaches Union law, s/he can expect to have an action brought against her/him in an appropriate national court under the doctrine of direct effect, with domestic courts being 'assisted' by the Court of Justice of the European Union under the preliminary reference procedure. (It should be remembered that the Court's role does not allow it to 'take over' the proceedings and its role is restricted to providing an interpretation of Union law and/or judgment as to the validity of legislative acts of the institutions.)

When a Member State breaches its obligations, the Treaty provides that the Commission or a second Member State may bring an action before the Court of Justice in order to ensure compliance. In addition, a Member State may find itself a defendant in an action before a national court under the doctrine of vertical direct effect and/or, where the claimant wishes to pursue an action for damages, under the principle of 'State damages' (*Francovich*). Often, Member States will find themselves the subject of an action brought by an individual in a national court, while at the same time being the subject of an enforcement action by the Commission.

Other than in actions relating to contractual liability, Union Institutions/ bodies will be brought before the European Court should they breach Union rules. Any challenge to the validity of legally effective acts of the institutions will normally be brought under Art 263 TFEU (judicial review), although due to the difficulties associated with proving *locus standi*, individuals should also consider the possibility of employing the preliminary reference, plea of illegality and/or 'action for damages' procedures to mount a challenge. Special notice should be taken of the differing effects of these actions, however.

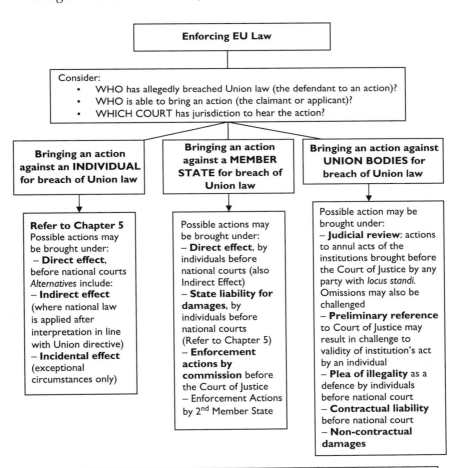

Enforcing EU Law

Consider:
- WHO has allegedly breached Union law (the defendant to an action)?
- WHO is able to bring an action (the claimant or applicant)?
- WHICH COURT has jurisdiction to hear the action?

Bringing an action against an INDIVIDUAL for breach of Union law	**Bringing an action against a MEMBER STATE for breach of Union law**	**Bringing an action against UNION BODIES for breach of Union law**
Refer to Chapter 5 Possible actions may be brought under: – **Direct effect,** before national courts *Alternatives* include: – **Indirect effect** (where national law is applied after interpretation in line with Union directive) – **Incidental effect** (exceptional circumstances only)	Possible actions may be brought under: – **Direct effect,** by individuals before national courts (also Indirect Effect) – **State liability for damages,** by individuals before national courts (Refer to Chapter 5) – **Enforcement actions by commission** before the Court of Justice – Enforcement Actions by 2nd Member State	Possible action may be brought under: – **Judicial review**: actions to annul acts of the institutions brought before the Court of Justice by any party with *locus standi*. Omissions may also be challenged – **Preliminary reference** to Court of Justice may result in challenge to validity of institution's act by an individual – **Plea of illegality** as a defence by individuals before national court – **Contractual liability** before national court – **Non-contractual damages**

Note: Individuals and States may also be subject to actions brought by the Commission as part of their role in ensuring fair competition within the EU (Arts 101–102 TFEU)

Enforcing EU Law

SOME ISSUES TO THINK ABOUT FURTHER:

- Which court(s) hear the majority of actions concerning Union law? Why is this?
- By what means can the acts of the Union's Institutions be challenged? What are the advantages and disadvantages of each? Does the TFEU encourage individuals to make such challenges?
- Through what means does the TFEU allow the Member States to be challenged for failure to comply with their EU obligations? Are there other means of challenging their compliance?

7 Free Movement of Goods

As previously discussed, the original European Communities were created in an attempt to ensure peace and economic stability within Europe, and the Treaties set out a number of aims to be achieved, through which these aspirations are to be fulfilled.

While, in the main, these aims may be categorised as economic, others have social impact, while others still can be said to be political in nature. *Economic* integration was, however, traditionally seen as the primary area of emphasis of the EEC and the objective of creating and maintaining an internal market remains a priority for the EU. Article 26 TFEU, in particular, provides that 'the internal market shall comprise an area without internal frontiers in which the free movement of goods, persons, services and capital is ensured'. These areas of 'free movement' have commonly become known as the 'four freedoms' and it is the first of these freedoms with which this chapter is primarily concerned.

Creating an area that has 'free movement of goods' cannot be achieved overnight and the rules concerning its creation and maintenance are often complex. Such rules can be best understood if an incremental approach is taken, and this chapter considers some of the more important rules which apply to Member States with regard to the removal of both pecuniary (monetary) and non-pecuniary (quantitative) barriers to trade.

Before moving on to consider the 'rules' relating to the internal market and the free movement of goods within it (Arts 26 to 37 TFEU), however, it is important to be clear about first, who such rules are aimed at and second, the meaning of the term 'goods'.

Reference to the relevant Treaty Articles makes it clear that this area of law is directed at the Member States. It is obvious that the free movement of goods is fundamental to the achievement of the EU's aims and the Court of Justice has consequently provided a wide interpretation of the term 'State', providing that not only public bodies come within its scope but also private bodies which receive public finances and are supervised by public authorities (Case 249/81, *Commission v Ireland*, 'Buy Irish' Campaign).

The term 'goods' is not defined by the Treaty and so again it has been necessary for the Court to consider exactly which goods may be subject to the EU's rules. Again the Court's interpretation is broad: in Case 7/68, *Commission v Italy* (the *1st Art Treasures* case), the Court defined 'goods' as including any product which can be valued in money and which is capable of forming the subject of a commercial transaction. It is relevant to note, however, that intangible benefits have been held not to come within this definition (Case C-97/98, *Jagerskiold v Gustafsson*).

I. THE ELIMINATION OF PECUNIARY (MONETARY) BARRIERS TO TRADE

It should be remembered that prior to the EEC's inception, each State levied customs duties on goods entering and leaving a particular territory. In order to create an area where trade was facilitated rather than hampered, customs duties had to be removed and a new system of regulation put into place.

1. The Customs Union and Common Customs Tariff (Arts 28 to 33 TFEU)

i. What the Treaty says

Article 28 TFEU provides that the Union 'shall comprise' a customs union. The creation of a customs union involves the removal of all customs duties, together with any charge having an equivalent effect to such a duty, on goods moving between States.

Article 28 TFEU also provides for the creation of a common customs tariff (CCT). The CCT is charged on all goods imported *into* the Union from non-Member States. It is charged at the same rate no matter which of the Member States the goods are imported into, or where they are exported from.

Articles 28 and 29 TFEU also make it clear that once imported goods have been subject to the CCT, they are considered to be in 'free circulation' and should be treated in exactly the same manner as goods originating within the EU. (This is the main difference between a customs union and a free trade area: in a free trade area goods from outside that area continue to be subject to different rules.) The CCT is a tariff raised by

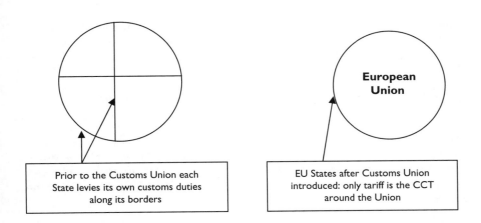

Prior to the Customs Union each State levies its own customs duties along its borders

EU States after Customs Union introduced: only tariff is the CCT around the Union

the EU, not the Member States, and as such forms part of the Union's budget. It should not, consequently, be confused with charges levied by the Member States as part of their own *internal* taxation systems (which are discussed in further detail below). The removal of existing customs duties was not, of course, achieved overnight and it was not until July 1968 that the final, remaining customs duties were removed and the CCT was introduced.

2. New customs duties and charges having equivalent effect (Art 30 TFEU)

The removal of existing customs duties has the obvious benefit of allowing trade to take place on a level playing field, allowing the consumer to be the final arbiter as to which goods will be successful and which less so. The levying of customs duties may, however, benefit Member States, allowing them an opportunity, for example, to promote domestically manufactured goods over imported goods through the imposition of high import taxes. Therefore, the possibility of a Member State imposing a *new* customs duty or similar charge cannot be ignored.

i. What the Treaty says

The removal of *existing* pecuniary barriers to trade would not, alone, have ensured the free movement of goods as it would not prevent Member States from re-erecting customs duties or putting into effect other charges having equivalent effect (CHEEs), in circumstances considered beneficial to that

State. Article 30 TFEU consequently provides that 'Customs duties on exports or any charges having equivalent effect shall be prohibited between Member States.'

ii. The Court of Justice's interpretation and application of Art 30

Article 30 TFEU – which applies to both imports and exports alike – appears to provide reasonably clear instruction to Member States, but it has still been necessary for the Court of Justice to interpret its exact meaning in order to ensure uniform application of its terms throughout the Union.

The Court has also made it clear that the purpose for which the duty or charge is levied is irrelevant and that it is the effect which is significant in deciding whether or not Art 30 applies (Case 24/68, *Commission v Italy*, the *2nd Art Treasures* case).

It has also been necessary for the Court to consider which charges will come within the scope of CHEEs. In the *2nd Art Treasures* case, the Court once again provided a wide definition, holding CHEEs to include 'any pecuniary charge ... imposed ... on domestic or foreign goods by reason of the fact that they cross a frontier'.

iii. The 'exceptions' to the rule

Once a duty or charge has been held to come within the scope of Art 30, it is immediately deemed to be unlawful; the Treaty provides for no derogation from its prohibitions. The Court of Justice has, however, explained that certain charges may not come within the scope of the Article. Such charges are those levied by a Member State for the provision of a service to an importer/exporter. By providing that such charges are outside the scope of Art 30, the Court of Justice has allowed Member States to recoup costs which would otherwise have to be borne by the State – which can be considered inappropriate if that State does not benefit but yet has to bear the cost. However, the case law generated by Court in regard to 'exceptions' has significantly complicated this area of law and it is recommended that the cases referred to below are read in order to get a better understanding of what is – or is not – within the scope of Art 30.

Before such a charge can be considered to be outside the scope of Art 30, a number of criteria must be fulfilled:

Charges levied for a service provided

Where a Member State has levied a charge for a service performed, that charge will not be considered to be a CHEE if the following criteria can be fulfilled (Case 24/68, *Commission v Italy*, the *Statistical Levy* case):

- the service rendered a specific benefit to the importer/exporter (*Statistical Levy* case);
- the charge is proportionate to quantity, not value or quality, of the goods to which the service has been rendered (Case 170/88, *Ford Espana v Spain*);
- the charge made for the service does not exceed its cost (Case 46/76, *Bauhuis*);
- no discrimination – both domestic and imported goods are treated alike (Case 87/75, *Bresciani*).

Charges levied in respect of an inspection

Where a Member State levies a charge for an inspection, it will not constitute a CHEE *provided* it can satisfy the following conditions (Case 18/87, *Commission v Germany*, the *Animal Inspection Fees* case):

- the inspection is mandatory under Union (or international) law (*Bauhuis*);
- the inspection is in the interest of the importer (*Bresciani*);
- the charge is proportionate to the quantity of the goods inspected and not their value or quality (*Bresciani*);
- the charge does not exceed the cost of the inspection (*Bauhuis*);
- the inspection is non-discriminatory (that is, both domestic and imported goods are treated alike) (Case 87/75, *Bresciani*);
- the inspection is in the interest of the Union and promotes the free movement of goods (*Animal Inspection Fees*).

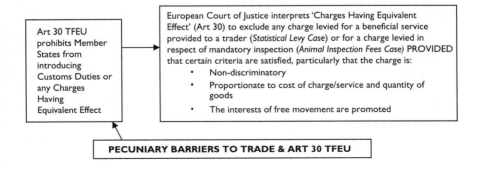

| Art 30 TFEU prohibits Member States from introducing Customs Duties or any Charges Having Equivalent Effect | European Court of Justice interprets 'Charges Having Equivalent Effect' (Art 30) to exclude any charge levied for a beneficial service provided to a trader (*Statistical Levy Case*) or for a charge levied in respect of mandatory inspection (*Animal Inspection Fees Case*) PROVIDED that certain criteria are satisfied, particularly that the charge is:
• Non-discriminatory
• Proportionate to cost of charge/service and quantity of goods
• The interests of free movement are promoted |

PECUNIARY BARRIERS TO TRADE & ART 30 TFEU

3. Discriminatory internal taxation (Arts 110 to 113 TFEU)

While prohibiting Member States from levying charges on goods as they move from State to State within the EU (Art 30 TFEU), the Treaty does not seek to deprive Member States of the right to levy *internal* taxes for the purpose of raising public revenue. A *genuine* internal tax can be described by reference to the well-used definition as 'a general system of internal dues applied systematically to categories of products in accordance with objective criteria irrespective of the origin of the products' (Case 90/79, *EC v France*). However, where an internal tax does not comply with this definition it will be prohibited and Art 110 can be seen as complementing the provisions contained in Art 30 TFEU.

It should be noted that the Court of Justice has made it clear that actions under Arts 30 and 110 TFEU are exclusive (that is, they are separate actions) but that it may at times be difficult to distinguish between 'charges' and unlawful 'internal taxation'. Consequently, actions should be brought before the Court together and the Court allowed to determine which should apply in any particular circumstances (Case 77/76, *Fratelli Cucchi*).

i. What the Treaty says

Article 110 TFEU provides that: 'No Member State shall impose, directly or indirectly, on the products of other Member States any internal taxation of any kind in excess of that imposed directly or indirectly on similar domestic products.' This means that internal taxation will be unlawful if it discriminates against imported products or is protective of domestic products.

ii. The European Court's interpretation of Art 110 TFEU

Clearly, there may be an argument as to what products may be considered to be 'similar'. In Case 27/67, *Fink-Frucht*, the Court of Justice provided that goods would be regarded as similar if they came within the same tax classification, but it has also been held that products need not necessarily be the same.

For example, in Case 170/78, *Commission v UK*, it was held that beer and wine were sufficiently similar to compete and it can be concluded that an appropriate test may be whether a consumer might *substitute* one product for the other for the purpose he has in mind. In Case 168/78, *Commission v France* (the *French Spirits* case), where France unsuccessfully attempted to distinguish alcoholic spirits made from grain and those made from fruit, characteristics such as composition, physical characteristics and consumer usage were considered.

iii. Indirectly discriminatory internal taxation

Taxation that is directly discriminatory overtly treats domestic and imported goods differently, but taxation that is indirectly discriminatory may, on the face of it, appear to comply with Union rules although, in reality, placing non-domestic goods at a disadvantage.

Case 112/84, *Humblot*, provides a helpful example of such treatment. French law decreed that the amount of car tax payable increased with the power rating of the vehicle, with cars below and above a 16CV rating being charged at different rates. No French car was rated above 16CV and therefore only imported cars fell into the higher tax rating. France's internal car taxation system was therefore considered to be covertly discriminatory and consequently unlawful under Art 110.

4. Enforcing the rules relating to pecuniary barriers to trade

Article 30 TFEU has been held to be directly effective (*Van Gend*). Traders may therefore enforce their rights against a Member State in the appropriate national court.

Member States will normally be required to repay any charges which have been unlawfully levied (Case 199/82, *Amministrazione delle Finanze*

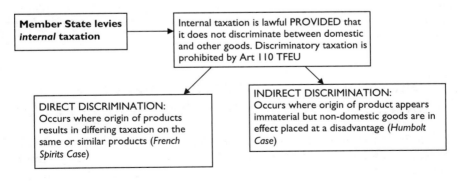

Unlawful Internal Taxation

dello Stato v San Giorgio), unless the trader has passed the costs on to his customers (Cases C-192–218/95, *Société Comateb*).

In addition, an errant State may find itself the subject of an enforcement action brought by either the Commission or another Member State, this time before the Court of Justice (Arts 226–228 TFEU, discussed in Chapter 6).

Article 110 TFEU is also directly effective (*Humblot*) and individuals may consequently enforce any rights accruing from the Article in their national courts. Once more, Member States who levy discriminatory internal taxation may also find themselves investigated by the Commission, as above.

II. THE ELIMINATION OF NON-PECUNIARY BARRIERS TO TRADE

1. The problem

The prohibition of *pecuniary* barriers to trade would not, alone, be sufficient to guarantee the free movement of goods within the EU. In addition to the pecuniary measures discussed above, measures of a non-pecuniary nature can also hinder free movement.

Non-pecuniary measures may include quantitative restrictions such as bans or quotas, while the imposition of compulsory inspections or trading rules relating to the composition, packaging and so on of goods are also capable of hindering trade. The Treaty consequently provides a prohibition on quantitative restrictions and measures having equivalent effect (MHEEs).

2. Quantitative restrictions and measures having equivalent effect (Arts 34 to 36 TFEU)

Article 34 TFEU provides that: 'Quantitative restrictions on *imports* and all measures having equivalent effect shall be prohibited between Member States.' Article 35 TFEU provides a similar prohibition with regard to exports.

Article 36 TFEU, on the other hand, provides an opportunity for Member States to derogate from the prohibitions in both Arts 34 and 35. The availability of such derogation – which may only be claimed in strictly limited circumstances – is a recognition that some issues are more important than the need to ensure the creation and maintenance of the internal market, allowing State regulation and the aim of free movement of goods to be reconciled.

As one would expect, each Member State has developed its own trading rules and, while the Union has attempted to harmonise such rules, progress has been slow. In the absence of harmonising legislation (where there has been such legislation, Arts 34 to 36 do not apply), the Court of Justice has taken the stance that national rules must not be allowed to hinder the free movement of goods, interpreting Arts 34 and 35 TFEU broadly to encompass as many restrictive measures as possible. On the other hand, Art 36 TFEU, which allows Member States to derogate, has been interpreted narrowly, ensuring that as few barriers to trade as possible exist.

i. Article 34 TFEU and imports

Whose 'measures' will be caught?

As has already been touched upon above, the Court has provided a wide interpretation with regard to whose measures may be caught by rules on free movement of goods, which is primarily addressed to Member States.

In Case 113/80, *Commission v Ireland* (the *Buy Irish* case), the Court of Justice held that the Irish Government's support of the Irish Goods Council's campaign was sufficient to allow the body to be considered 'public' for the purposes of Art 34, while in Case C-265/95, *Commission v France*, the Court went even further by declaring that the actions of French farmers, who had disrupted imports, came within the ambit of the French Government, as the State authorities were considered not to have taken sufficient action to ensure free movement: in other words, an *omission* may also be considered to be an MHEE.

Meaning of 'quantitative restrictions'

Quantitative restrictions (QRs) can be described as national measures which impose a numerical limit on goods of a particular type entering a domestic market. The purpose of such behaviour is often to offer protection to domestic products. The Court has provided that 'total or partial restraints' on trade fall within the scope of the term (Case 2/73, *Geddo*), thus making it clear that quotas and total bans on goods are prohibited. (It needs to be emphasised that the ban or quota must relate to goods and not to something related to the goods. If, for example, an additive is banned this is not a QR, as the goods – without the additive – would not be outlawed.)

Meaning of 'measures having equivalent effect'

As well as prohibiting quantitative restrictions, Art 34 outlaws MHEEs. This term has proved difficult to define and has been the subject of both secondary legislation and numerous interpretations by the Court of Justice. In general terms, MHEEs can be seen as measures that discriminate by, for example, promoting or favouring domestic goods (Case 249/81, *Commission v Ireland*, the *Buy Irish* case) or which make importation of goods more difficult or costly (Case 50/85, *Schloh*).

Commission Directive 70/50/EEC (OJ 1097 L13/29)

Commission Directive 70/50/EEC (OJ 1097 L13/29) was adopted in an attempt to amplify the meaning of Art 34 TFEU and, although no longer in force, it is still used as a guide to the practices which are prohibited by Arts 34 and 35. The Directive makes a distinction between two types of measures:

(a) measures which apply only to imports and are therefore discriminatory: known in 'Euro-speak' as distinctly applicable measures (DAMs); and

(b) measures which are applicable to both domestic and imported products alike and which therefore are not overtly discriminatory: known as indistinctly applicable measures (IDAMs).

The Commission, by means of Art 2(1) of the Directive, concluded that while discriminatory measures (DAMs) would *always* come within the scope of Arts 34 and would consequently be prohibited, IDAMs (unless provided with a derogation under Art 36 TFEU, discussed below) would not normally come within the scope of Art 34 unless they placed an additional burden on imports.

Judicial development of the meaning of 'measures having equivalent effect'

The Court's jurisprudence has been responsible for developing Art 34 into a formidable tool in the drive against national trading rules that restrict the free movement of goods. In an attempt to illustrate this development, the Court's decisions will be considered in chronological order.

The *Dassonville* 'Formula'

While Directive 70/50/EEC provided that IDAMs (non-directly discriminatory measures) do not normally come within the scope of Art 34, the Court of Justice has held in Case 8/74, *Procureur du Roi v Dassonville*, that:

All trading rules enacted by Member States which are capable of hindering directly or indirectly, actually or potentially, intra-Community trade are to be considered as measures having an effect equivalent to quantitative restrictions.

In what has become the authoritative definition of an MHEE, the Court interpreted Art 34 extremely broadly, bringing both discriminatory as well as apparently neutral measures within its scope. In *Dassonville*, the Court also provided that it is not necessary to show an actual effect on trade between Member States – it is sufficient to show that the measure is *capable* of such an effect. This is a particularly all-encompassing interpretation, allowing Member States very little autonomy in regard to their trading rules. (This broad definition is hardly surprising, however, given that the Court's usual approach is to ensure that any barriers to the achievement of the aims of the Union be removed.)

Cassis and the 'Rule of Reason' (The First *Cassis* Principle)

In Case 120/78, *Rewe-Zentral v Bundesmonopolverwaltung fur Branntwein* (the *Cassis de Dijon* case), the Court of Justice qualified the above approach by applying a 'Rule of Reason'. The Court held that, in the absence of EU harmonisation legislation, where the measure in question is an IDAM (i.e. not *directly* discriminatory), it *may* be justified and therefore not come within the scope of Art 34, *provided* that the measure is:

(a) 'necessary' (i.e. its aim cannot be achieved through less restrictive means: also known as *proportionality*) in order to satisfy

(b) a 'mandatory requirement'. (This term can perhaps be better understood when considering Case C-120/95, *Decker*, where the Court substituted the term 'overriding reason in the general interest' for 'mandatory'.)

The Court went on to list particular areas where this may occur, in particular:

- the effectiveness of fiscal supervision;
- the protection of public health;
- the fairness of commercial transactions;
- consumer protection.

This list is not exhaustive, however, and the Court of Justice has shown itself willing to extend the areas which have included:

- the promotion of national culture (Cases 60 and 61/84, *Cinéthèque v Federation des Cinemas Francais*);
- protection of the environment (Case 302/86, *Commission v Denmark*, the *Danish Bottles* case); and more recently
- fundamental rights (Case C-112/00, *Schmidberger v Austria*).

Prior to the introduction of the 'Rule of Reason' in *Cassis*, it was thought that all measures caught within the very broad '*Dassonville* formula' would be prohibited by Art 34 *unless* they could be justified under Art 36 TFEU (discussed below). Following *Cassis*, it could be concluded that *non*-discriminatory measures will not come within Art 34, provided they could fulfil the criteria set out above. Further, it is relevant to note that it will be for the *national* court to determine whether the 'Rule of Reason' applies to a particular national rule (Case 145/88, *Torfaen v B&Q*).

The distinction between 'selling arrangements' and 'product requirements': the judgment in *Keck and Mithouard*

Due to confusion over the exact scope of Art 34 (and the consequent high volume of cases coming before national courts and the Court of Justice through the preliminary reference/ruling procedure under Art 267 TFEU) in Cases C-267 and 268/91, *Keck and Mithouard*, the Court took the opportunity to 're-examine and clarify' its case law relating to MHEEs.

In addition to confirming the *Dassonville* formula, the Court held that 'contrary to what has previously been decided ... certain selling arrangements' were outside the scope of the *Dassonville* formula, *provided* that they applied 'to all affected traders operating within the national territory and provided they affect in the same manner, in law and in fact, the marketing of domestic products and those from other Member States'. Simplified, this means that:

(a) *certain* past decisions of the Court may no longer be 'good' law; and

(b) 'selling arrangements', if *non*-discriminatory in nature and in effect, are outside the scope of Art 34 TFEU.

While the Court's judgment was intended to clarify the law, it caused a certain amount confusion, particularly in regard to the exact nature of 'selling arrangements'. The Court's judgment can be concluded, however, as distinguishing between national measures which:

- relate to goods themselves, that is their *intrinsic* qualities, such as composition, size, labelling, packaging, weight, form and so on, known as 'product requirements', which continued to be prohibited; and

- relate to *extrinsic* qualities such as advertising, who may sell goods or where or when goods may be sold, which are 'selling arrangements' and which will only be prohibited if they have the potential to hinder trade.

The later judgment in Case C-368/95, *Familiapress*, is helpful in terms of understanding how the concept of a lawful 'selling arrangement' is applied by the Court. In this case a German company published a magazine offering, as a marketing tool, competitions involving prizes. The publication was also distributed in Austria, which had a trading rule imposing a ban on such competitions in the press – activities which were permitted under German law. A preliminary reference to the Court of Justice on the question of whether this Austrian rule was contrary to Art 34 (then Art 30 TEC) was made and the Court considered whether the national ban was a 'selling arrangement' and therefore outside the scope of Art 34. In para 11 of its judgment, the Court provided:

> that, even though the relevant national legislation is directed against a method of sales promotion, in this case it bears on the actual content of the products, in so far as the competitions in question form an integral part of the magazine in which they appear. As a result, the national legislation in question as applied to the facts of the case is not concerned with a selling arrangement within the meaning of the judgment in *Keck and Mithouard*.

Consequently, even though the national ban on competitions appeared to relate to marketing, which would suggest it was a 'selling arrangement', the competitions were held to be part of the composition of the magazine as the magazine would have had to have been altered in order to comply with Austrian law: the national ban was consequently prohibited by Art 34.

Keck can therefore be seen as an important case in explaining that certain national trading rules (i.e. selling arrangements), in addition to those held to be outside the scope of Art 34 by *Cassis*, will not be prohibited – but only if non-discriminatory in both law and fact.

Recognising discriminatory rules: discrimination 'in law and in fact'
As has already been discussed, there is little doubt that national measures which directly discriminate between domestic goods and imported goods are prohibited by Art 34 TFEU. The Court of Justice has, however, made it absolutely clear that even indistinctly applicable national measures (which *appear* to apply to both domestic and imported goods in the same manner) may come within the definition of an MHEE due to their actual (negative) impact on the free movement of goods.

Measures which amount to a 'dual burden' on importers
Such indirectly discriminatory measures are sometimes referred to as measures which create a *dual burden* for the importer, by placing an additional encumbrance on imported goods – as did the national rule in the *Cassis* case, which required all Cassis sold in Germany to contain an alcohol level as set by the State, which consequently put an additional burden on

all importers of the liquor from States where no such rule applied as their goods had to be modified before they could be lawfully traded.

Measures which impede market access

The 'dual burden' rule has since been further developed by the Court of Justice in later cases. If an apparently neutral measure has the potential to impede the market access of imported goods it will be prohibited. In Case C-412/93, *Leclerc Siplec*, AG Jacobs contended that where a national rule which *directly and substantially impeded the access of an imported product to a national market*, that rule should be regarded as an MHEE.

In Cases C-34 to 36/95, *De Agostini*, for example, which related to a Swedish ban on advertising aimed at young children, the Court of Justice provided that the ban was prohibited by Art 34, despite on the face of it appearing to be non-discriminatory. This was because the national rule had a greater impact on the market access of imported goods, as, if the goods could not be advertised, they would have no means of becoming 'known' by consumers in the importing State.

Similarly, in Case C-405/98, *Konsumentombudsmannen v Gourmet International Products* (the *Gourmet Foods* case), Swedish law prohibited the advertising of alcoholic beverages in trade magazines. While this rule was again not directly discriminatory, being targeted at both domestic and non-domestic products alike, it was successfully argued that it had a far more detrimental effect on (the less well-known) non-domestic brands than on domestic brands. It was consequently determined to be an MHEE despite, at first sight, appearing to be a non-discriminatory 'selling arrangement' saved by the '*Keck* principle'.

Discrimination and 'use restrictions'

More recently the Court of Justice has considered national rules which restrict the *use* of goods: that is, while there may be no restrictions on the entry of the product, there are limitations on the use that products may be put to in the State. Two cases are instructive here.

In Case C-142/05, *Mickelson v Ross*, the Court held that a restriction on where goods (in this case jet skis) may be used was an MHEE and within the scope of Art 34, although in this instance the national rule was justified under Art 36 TFEU.

Similarly, in Case C-110/05, *Commission v Italy*, following the Italian State introducing legislation that prohibited motorcycles from towing a trailer, the Court held that the rule hindered the market access of such trailers (who would consider purchase if their use was limited?) and was, as such, a breach of Art 34 TFEU, although once more the national rule was justified under Art 36.

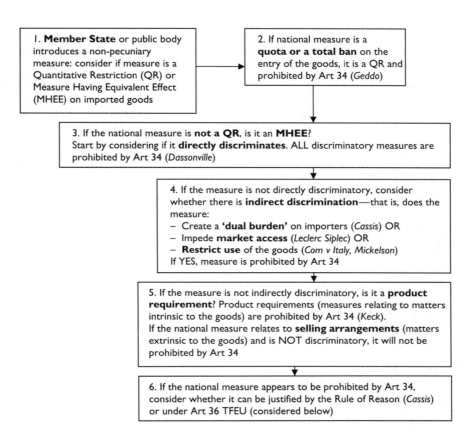

Free Movement of Goods: Applying Article 34 TFEU

It can be seen from the case law of the Court of Justice, the Court is keen to eliminate *any* national laws that have a restrictive impact on the movement of goods within the Union.

ii. Article 35 TFEU and exports

There may be instances, although less frequent than in relation to imports, where a Member State may wish to restrict the free flow of exports and consequently the EU has responded to such a possibility.

Article 35 TFEU prohibits quantitative restrictions and all MHEEs on *exported* goods. While the prohibition contained within Art 35 *appears* to mirror that contained within Art 34 TFEU, this is not actually the case.

This is because the case law of the Court of Justice in decisions such as *Dassonville, Cassis* and *Keck* related to the Court's interpretation of Art 34 and *not* Art 35.

While Art 34 has been held to prohibit both DAMs (discriminatory measures) and IDAMs (measures which treat domestic and other goods alike), it would appear that Art 35 only prohibits measures which discriminate (DAMs) (Case 15/79, *Groenveld*).

Examples of measures that have been held to be MHEEs with regard to exports include Case 237/82, *Jongeneel Kaas v Netherlands*, where inspection documents were required for exports while no such requirement was placed on goods destined for the domestic market. Also, in Case C-5/94, *R v MAFF ex p Lomas*, where national authorities refused to sanction the export of live animals to States where slaughterhouse standards were not thought to be adequate, the Court held that such a national rule was within Art 35 TFEU and therefore prohibited.

3. Derogation from the prohibitions contained in Arts 34 and 35: Art 36 TFEU

i. What the Treaty says

The EU has recognised that certain measures put into effect by Member States, although detrimental to free movement of goods, may be necessary to fulfil important functions. In order to give effect to the recognition that the positive effects of certain measures outweigh the negative effects on trade, Art 36 TFEU provides that:

> The provisions of Arts 34 and 35 shall not preclude prohibitions or restrictions on imports, exports or goods in transit justified on grounds of:
> * public morality;
> * public security or public policy;
> * protection of the health and life of humans, animals or plants;
> * protection of national treasures possessing artistic, historic or archaeological value;
> * protection of industrial and commercial property.

The Article goes on to qualify this, providing that: 'Such prohibitions or restrictions shall not, however, constitute a means of arbitrary discrimination or a disguised restriction on trade between Member States.'

ii. The jurisprudence of the Court of Justice

The principle of 'mutual recognition' (the Second *Cassis* Principle)

The starting point in considering whether a national measure is indeed lawful was developed in the *Cassis* Case. In Case 120/78, *Rewe-Zentral v Bundesmonopolverwaltung fur Branntwein* (the *Cassis de Dijon* case), the Court of Justice developed a second, highly important principle. The Court provided that, in the absence of harmonising legislation, there should be a *presumption* by Member States that goods which have been *lawfully* produced and marketed in one Member State will comply with the minimum requirements of the importing State, thereby limiting the need for an importing State to enact trading rules requiring certain additional standards to be met or inspections to be undertaken, for example.

The presumption can, however, be *rebutted* by evidence that further measures are necessary to ensure adequate standards are met (Case 18/84, *Commission v France*).

The principle has also been of fundamental importance to the process of harmonisation of trading rules within the EU. In order to create an integrated market, the Union recognises that trading rules within the Member States must be in harmony with one another and the Commission has since supported the principle, providing that:

> Any product imported from another Member State must in principle be admitted to the territory of the importing Member State if it has been lawfully produced, that is, conforms to rules and processes of manufacture that are customarily and traditionally accepted in the exporting country, and is marketed in the territory of another. (Commission Communication OJ 1980 256/2)

In addition, as the Member States should not automatically treat imported goods with suspicion, the need for national rules relating to the *quality* of imported goods can therefore be kept to a minimum.

The general position of the Court of Justice

As touched upon earlier, the Court of Justice has adopted a narrow stance with regard to its interpretation of the measures which may enjoy derogation from the prohibitions found under Arts 34 and 35 TFEU, as to do otherwise could constitute a threat to the Union's fundamental principle of free movement of goods.

It should be remembered that Art 36 TFEU cannot be used to justify a measure in areas which have been subject to harmonisation by the EU.

iii. Grounds for derogation under Art 36 TFEU

As already touched upon, the Treaty provides an exhaustive list of grounds under which a Member State may claim derogation from the prohibitions provided by Arts 34 and 35 TFEU. The Court has generally expressed unwillingness to consider any extension of these grounds, as it sees this as a matter for legislation (as evidenced by the Court's dicta in Case 113/80, *Commission v Ireland*, the *Irish Souvenirs* case). Prior to the *Cassis* judgment (the 'Rule of Reason', discussed above), Art 36 was the only means of 'saving' a prohibited measure from being outlawed under Art 34. (Art 36 TFEU is still the only means under which a measure prohibited under Art 34 TFEU may be 'saved', as the 'Rule of reason' does not apply to Art 35.)

Public morality

Consideration of Case 34/79, *R v Henn and Darby* and Case 121/85, *Conegate Ltd v HM Customs & Excise*, provide examples of the Court's interpretation of this ground.

In *Henn and Darby*, the defendants were accused by UK authorities of illegally importing pornographic material. They argued, in their defence, that UK rules contravened Art 34. The Court of Justice found that the UK's ban on pornography was justified under Art 36, as it is for each State to determine the standards of public morality that exist within its own territory.

In *Conegate*, the defendants imported inflatable, life-size 'love dolls' into the UK. The dolls were seized and, once more, it was argued that the UK rules constituted a threat to trade. The UK rules did not contain a similar ban on the domestic manufacture of 'love dolls' and, although the Court repeated its dicta from *Henn and Darby*, it was held that a State may not rely on Art 36 'when its legislation contains no prohibition on the manufacture or marketing of the same goods in its territory'.

What can be concluded from these decisions is that, while the Member States are free to determine their own moral standards, they must not place any stricter burden on imported goods than they do on nationally produced goods.

Public policy

Case 7/78, *R v Thompson and Others* is a rare example of a successful action under this ground, involving the right to mint (and melt down) coinage.

The Court held that this ground could be successful where there is a need to protect a right that is traditionally regarded as involving a fundamental interest of the State.

Public security

This ground often goes hand in hand with a claim based on public policy. In Case 72/83, *Campus Oil Ltd v Minister for Industry and Energy*, importers of petroleum products were required to buy 35 per cent of their oil from the Irish National Petroleum Company at a fixed price. The Court of Justice accepted that this was to enable the Irish Government to maintain a viable refinery that could meet essential needs in times of crisis and that the national measure could be justified as in the interests of public security. The Court has also held that both external and internal security comes within the scope of this derogation (Case C-367/89, *Richardt*).

Protection of health and life of humans, animals or plants

This is the area most claimed by Member States in order to justify obstacles to trade. The Court of Justice has made it clear that, when considering whether or not a measure may be justified, there are a number of issues that are likely to be relevant to its deliberations, primarily:

- in the absence of harmonising legislation, the principle of 'mutual recognition' may be relevant. This principle is discussed in further detail above but, to briefly recap, it provides that goods lawfully produced in one Member State should be presumed to reach minimum requirement standards in all Member States (*Cassis*);
- scientific or other relevant knowledge (Case 174/82, *Officier van Justitie v Sandoz* and Case 178/84, *Commission v Germany*, the *German Beer* case, including the existence of a technical need);
- in a case involving inspections or checks in Case 4/75, *Rewe-Zentralfinanz v Landschwirtschaftskammer* (*San José Scale*), it was held that inspections will only be justified if imported products constitute a real risk not present in comparable domestic goods, while in Case 228/91, *Commission v Italy*, the Court provided that where health certificates are available, spot checks, rather than continual inspection, will be acceptable.

It should be evident that an overlap exists between measures justifiable under the 'Rule of Reason' (*Cassis*) and Art 34, particularly in the area of 'public health'. However, when Member States have previously sought to justify measures on public health grounds, the Court has chosen to consider such requests under Art 34.

Protection of national treasures

There is a paucity of definitive case law in this area and therefore little guidance as to what will be considered to be a 'national treasure' (although Directive 93/7/EEC and Regulation EEC No 3911/92 have been used to assist). Restrictions on the export of artefacts have been generally considered justifiable but in the *1st Art Treasures* case, which was brought as a result of Italy's breach of Art 30 TFEU rather than Art 34, the European Court failed to allow the Italian Government to levy an export tax on 'cultural artefacts' in an attempt to restrict their removal abroad.

Protection of industrial or commercial property

Industrial or commercial property (also known as 'intellectual property') rights may take the form of trade marks, copyright, patents and so on. Protection of such rights encourages innovation and their ownership is complemented by Art 345 TFEU, which provides that: 'The Treaty shall in no way prejudice the rules in Member States governing the system of property ownership.'

Where national rules allow such rights to be protected, an individual with an intellectual property right (IPR) can often rely on such legislation to prevent re-importation of particular goods. National legislation relating to an IPR may, however, have the result of restricting trade, which is, of course, prohibited under Union law.

The Court of Justice has struck a balance between the protection of an IPR and the principle of free movement of goods by distinguishing between the existence of an IPR and the exercise of such rights. The Court has provided that an IPR will be protected by Art 36 only when rights have not been exhausted by the subject matter of the right being put into free circulation within the EU (Case 15/74, *Centrafarm v Sterling Drug*). This is probably best understood by the provision of the following example.

An inventor (A) has patented a new invention and so an IPR exists. Should A decide to award a licence to manufacturer B, giving B the right to produce the invention, A will be said to have *exercised* his IPRs.

If the product remains within the Member State, the rights afforded by the award of a patent will be subject to the intellectual property laws of that Member State only and EU rules will be irrelevant.

If, however, the product is exported by B, A will not be able to exert any further control over the product, even if it is re-imported, as the EU provides that his rights were *exhausted* or 'used up' when he awarded B authority over the product.

The doctrine of exhaustion of rights has been held to be applicable to:

- patents – Case 15/74, *Centrafarm v Sterling Drug*;
- trade marks – Case 16/74, *Centrafarm v Winthrop*;
- copyright – Case 78/70, *Deutsche Grammophon v Metro*.

It should be noted that a certain amount of secondary legislation has been adopted by the Union with the aim of harmonising the rules in this area and such legislation, although outside the scope of this book, may need to be considered.

iv. The matter of 'arbitrary discrimination'

Article 36 specifically provides that 'prohibitions or restrictions shall not, however, constitute a means of arbitrary discrimination'. An example of such discrimination can be found in Case 152/78, *Commission v France*. In this case French advertising restrictions appeared to be biased against grain-based spirits, while favouring fruit-based spirits. The French authorities attempted to justify this on the grounds of 'public health', arguing that grain-based spirits were more likely to be injurious to health. Independent evidence, however, proved the effect on health of both spirits to be identical. (Interestingly, the French produce fruit-based spirits, while grain-based spirits are generally imported. The Court, in its judgment, considered the restriction to be capricious, constituting arbitrary discrimination.)

v. Measures which are a 'disguised restriction on trade'

In addition to 'arbitrary discrimination' being outlawed, Art 36 also provides that national measures must not constitute a 'disguised restriction on trade'. An example of such behaviour can be found in Case 40/82, *Commission v UK* (the *Newcastle Disease* case) in which the UK banned the import of poultry and poultry products from States which did not have a policy of slaughtering flocks of birds with Newcastle disease. The UK attempted to justify this on the grounds of 'health'. Evidence showed that other methods of controlling the disease were equally effective and that the ban had been imposed following pressure from UK poultry producers relating to an increase in turkeys imported from France and Ireland. Furthermore, when French importers complied with UK requirements, additional restrictions were imposed. The Court of Justice concluded that the UK's restrictions therefore amounted to a disguised restriction on trade.

vi. The requirement of 'proportionality'

Although not specifically mentioned in Art 36 TFEU, it is implicit that the General Principle of proportionality will apply to any measure for which a Member State is claiming justification. The principle requires that measures be no more than strictly necessary to achieving a particular aim (Case 124/81, *Commission v UK, Re UHT Milk*). Consequently, it should always be considered whether or not the aim of a national measure can be achieved by less restrictive means.

Justification under Art 36 TFEU: Derogation from the prohibition contained in Arts 34 and 35

'Cassis' and Mutual Recognition:

The Court of Justice has provided that goods lawfully produced in one MS should be presumed to comply with minimum requirements in all MSs.

This is seen as a **starting point** in regard to the Free Movement of Goods

---

A national measure that appears to be prohibited by either Art 34 or 35 TFEU MAY obtain derogation (may be justified) if Art 36 applies: A derogation may be obtained on the following grounds:

GROUNDS:

Exhaustive and interpreted narrowly by the Court of Justice, grounds are as follows:

– Public morality (*Henn & Darby* and *Conegate*)
– Public policy (*Thompson*)
– Public security (*Campus Oil*)
– Protection of health & life of humans, animals & plants: an often-claimed derogation to which 'mutual recognition' closely applies. Consider the state of scientific knowledge (*Sandoz & the German Beer case*) and the need for inspections (*San Jose Scale*) and health certificates (*Com v Italy*)
– Protection of National Treasures (*Art Treasures case*)
– Protection of Industrial/Commercial Property Consider the Exhaustion of Rights

In addition to finding the appropriate ground, the national measure must not be:

– **Arbitrary** discrimination or a **disguised restriction** on trade (consider the *Newcastle Disease Case*), and must be

– **Proportionate**: Consider whether the aim of the measure could be achieved in a less restrictive manner (*Cassis*)

– A measure will not be justified in an area which has been the subject of EU **harmonising legislation**

III. CONCLUSIONS

Students who have survived this far will probably agree with a comment made at the beginning of this chapter, that is, the rules relating to the free movement of goods are complex! Remember that understanding why the rules have been developed in the first place and adopting a logical, incremental approach in regard to this area of law will allow you to master its intricacies.

SOME ISSUES TO THINK ABOUT FURTHER:

- Why are rights in regard to the free movement of goods interpreted broadly, yet limitation on those lights interpreted restrictively by the Court of Justice?
- Has the Court of Justice changed its interpretation of 'measures having equivalent effect to quantitative restrictions on imports' since its decision in *Dassonville*?
- Why is Art 36 TFEU not applicable in areas which have been subject to harmonising measures?

8 Free Movement of Persons

As already considered in previous chapters, economic integration between the Member States has always been a central theme of the EU. In order to ensure that this aim is achieved, the TFEU provides that all obstacles to the free movement of goods, persons, services and capital be abolished within the EU (Art 26 TFEU).

Free movement of persons is considered to be fundamental to the creation of the internal market: without a mobile workforce, workers would not, for example, be able to move around the Union to fill manpower or skills shortages. Similarly, European entrepreneurs would not be able to expand their businesses into new States, nor service providers cross the borders to provide occasional services to clients in other Member States! The consequences of such occurrences would obviously be detrimental to the creation of an integrated EU. Unsurprisingly therefore, the TFEU gives all Union citizens the basic right to move from their home State to another Union State (the 'host' State), largely unhampered by unnecessary restrictions or discrimination based on nationality.

Simple as this may initially appear, *specific* rights in regard to free movement within the EU are dependent on categorising the status of individuals (and businesses) wishing to move between States. 'Status' largely depends on two things: nationality and occupational activity. While Art 21 TFEU provides all Union citizens with an outline of their rights to free movement, Arts 45 to 62 TFEU provide a framework of rights for those who are economically active. The rights contained within the Treaty have been further expanded by secondary legislation and developed by the jurisprudence of the Court of Justice. EU citizens, employees, the self-employed, family members and businesses all enjoy rights but their *exact* nature – and source – depends on the group into which an individual falls. While each 'group' is touched on below, albeit briefly in regard to the self-employed, establishment and the provision of services, the main emphasis of this chapter is placed on the rights of workers and citizens.

In addition to providing rights of free movement, the EU has attempted to abolish checks at internal borders, and most Member States (but not the UK) have now signed the Schengen Agreement, which attempts to achieve this. In reality, however, the variety of languages spoken within the EU undoubtedly has an adverse effect on cross-border mobility. Tethered largely by linguistic differences, it is instructive to note that no more than 1 per cent of EU citizens live outside their country of origin.

I. GAINING THE RIGHT TO 'MOVE FREELY'

1. The importance of EU citizenship

The provision of rights of free movement does not only have economic implications, of course, and the social aspects of such rights are also important. Indeed, the concept of free movement of persons has changed significantly over the years. Originally, because they were seen as factors of production in the same way as, for example, raw materials, only those who were economically active, such as employees and the self-employed, were allowed rights of free movement. However, others – in their relatively new guise as European citizens – now have rights independent of their economic status. (It should be noted that the rights of EU citizens are not limited to free movement within the EU. It is consequently advisable to refer to the Treaty, particularly Part Two of the TFEU, for further detail on this, although matters relating to democracy and the participation of citizens in the political life of the Union can also be found in the TEU.)

i. The importance of citizenship of the EU

It is essential to emphasise at the outset that rights relating to free movement are only *directly* provided to citizens of the EU. This is demonstrated by Art 21 TFEU, which provides that: 'Every citizen of the Union shall have the right to move and reside freely within the territory of the Member States.' (It should also be noted, however, that the Treaty Article, although held to have direct effect (Case C-413/99, *Baumbast*) provides that such rights are 'subject to the limitations and conditions laid down by the Treaties and by the measures adopted to give them effect' and such rights are, consequently, subject to certain constraints, discussed later.)

ii. Who can be considered to be a citizen of the Union?

Originally introduced by the ToA in an attempt to strengthen ties between the EU and its citizens, Art 20 TFEU (then Art 17 TEC) established the concept of Union citizenship, providing that: 'Every person holding the nationality of a Member State shall be a citizen of the Union.' Consequently, only those holding the nationality of one of the Member States are EU citizens and only they have *direct* access to rights and benefits relating to free movement.

This does not mean that nationals of non-EU States have no rights under Union law. Indeed, non-EU *family members* of Union citizens will, for example, normally enjoy rights indirectly through their relationship to an EU citizen (sometimes referred to as 'piggy-back' rights), although it is important to understand that *the EU citizen must first have exercised their right of free movement* before their family members may enjoy such rights (Case C-127/08, *Metock*). The specific rights of family members are further considered below.

iii. What of non-EU citizens who are not 'family members' of an EU citizen?

Title V of the TFEU attempts to provide and safeguard the rights of non-EU nationals in regard to matters such as visas, immigration and asylum. As yet, however, no coherent body of EU rules governing the treatment of non-EU citizens within the Union has been developed and so their rights are, in the main, the subject of national rather than EU law, taking this matter outside the scope of this text.

iv. Citizens' rights to move freely

Once it has been established that a person wishing to enjoy rights of free movement is a Union citizen, in order to clarify the exact nature and, importantly, the exact *source* of their rights, it is necessary to determine their *status*. This is because, as touched on above, Union law differentiates between different categories of EU citizen, with the TFEU largely concentrating on the provision of rights for those who are economically active, and secondary legislation normally providing rights to those Union citizens who are not.

2. Free movement of 'economically active' persons

The TFEU differentiates between categories of economic activity, namely:

- *employment/workers' rights*: Arts 45 to 48 TFEU relate to the rights of wage and salary earners to take up employment – and permanent residence – in a host State;

- *self-employment/establishment*: Arts 49 to 55 TFEU relate to the rights of the self-employed and businesses to establish a permanent base in a host State;

- *service providers*: Arts 56 to 62 TFEU relate to the right to enter a host State in order to provide services without, normally, setting up a permanent base in the host State.

In addition, the TFEU also contains other provisions which underpin the free movement of persons, including Art 18, which provides a general prohibition on discrimination on the grounds of nationality, which should always be read in conjunction with free movement rights.

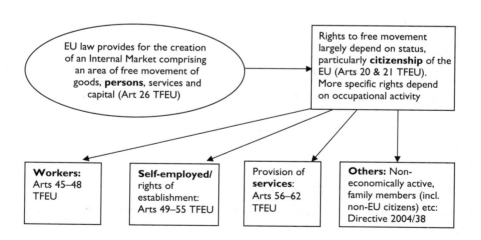

Overview of Free Movement of Persons

II. FREE MOVEMENT: WORKERS' RIGHTS (ARTS 45–48 TFEU)

As explained above, the Treaty provisions already highlighted have been expanded upon by secondary legislation (largely Directive 2004/38 and Regulation 1612/68), and both primary and secondary legislation has been subject to extensive interpretation by the Court of Justice. (While earlier secondary legislation on the free movement of persons within the EU was repealed in April 2006, it is likely that the case law relating to this will still remain relevant to Directive 2004/38, as the newer legislation was largely consolidating in nature.)

1. The meaning of the term 'worker'

i. Legislation

Neither the Treaty nor secondary legislation attempt to provide a definition of the term 'worker'.

ii. Case law of the Court of Justice

The Court of Justice has made it clear that 'worker' is a Union concept and that the Court alone has jurisdiction to define the term (Case 75/63, *Hoekstra (née Unger) v BBDA*). This ensures that the Member States cannot restrict rights by developing a narrow definition. While case law makes it clear that 'worker' generally refers to an employed person, the term has been interpreted very widely, allowing as many citizens as possible to enjoy the rights provided – thus promoting free movement.

The following decisions provide a flavour of the Court's broad and inclusive interpretation of 'worker':

o Case 75/63, *Hoekstra (née Unger) v BBDA* – a worker who had lost his job but was capable of finding another should be considered a worker;

o Case 53/81, *Levin v Staatssecretaris* – a part-time employee is to be considered a worker, provided the work is 'real' or genuine work of an economic nature and not nominal or minimal;

o Case 139/85, *Kempf v Staatssecretaris van Justitie* – a part-time music teacher (from Germany), even though in receipt of supplementary benefit (in the Netherlands) to bring his wage up to minimum levels, came within the term;

- Case 196/87, *Steymann v Staatssecretaris van Justitie* – a member of a religious community provided with his 'keep' and pocket money, but not formal wages, was held to be a worker;
- Case 344/87, *Bettray v Staatssecretaris van Justitie* – an important case demonstrating the *limits* of the term 'worker'. It was held that, as the position was artificially created by the Government as part of a drug rehabilitation programme, he could not be considered to be engaged in 'economic activity' of a 'genuine' nature.

iii. Job seekers

Case C-292/89, *R v Immigration Appeal Tribunal ex p Antonissen* – although not directly relating to the definition of 'worker', this decision provides that an individual who is seeking and has a genuine chance of finding work should be allowed to enter and remain for a reasonable amount of time. This has now been confirmed by Art 14 and developed by Art 6, of Directive 2004/38, which provides that any Union citizen may reside in a host State for up to three months without the usual formalities, providing they have a passport or a valid identity card, which includes job seekers.

It should be noted, however, that the rights of those searching for work are *not* as extensive as those of a worker, as is made clear by Art 14 of the Directive, and host States are not, for example, bound to provide social assistance during this three-month period.

2. Basic rights afforded to workers by the TFEU

Article 45 TFEU contains the principal provisions relating to migrant workers. These include:

- the right to accept offers of employment actually made and to move freely within the host State for this purpose;
- the right to reside in the host State, for the purpose of employment, under the same rules as enjoyed by nationals; and
- the right to remain in the host State after having been employed in that State (following retirement or incapacity).

3. The rights of exit, entry and residence of workers

Article 45 TFEU, as outlined above, mentions in overview the right of residence and the right to remain in a host State. It is silent, however, on the right to exit a home State and enter a host State. Consequently, secondary legislation expands upon the rules.

i. Extension of rights relating to exit, entry and residence

The rights provided by the Treaty have been extended and expanded by secondary legislation. Articles 4 and 5 of Directive 2004/38 EC relate to rights concerned with exiting a home State and entering a host State.

In order to ensure that a home State cannot deny exit to key workers, Art 4 provides that nationals must be provided with a passport or identity card, while the Directive further provides that a host State cannot create a barrier to free movement by making it prohibitively difficult for migrant workers to enter a host State, by demanding entry visas or other such documents (Art 5, Directive 2004/38).

While *all EU citizens* normally have the right to reside in a host State for up to three months, irrespective of their status or wealth, a worker will have the right to reside after this period, although this may be subject to a requirement to register with the relevant authorities of the host State (Art 8, Directive 2004/38). The right of *permanent* residency becomes available to those who have legally resided for a continuous period of *five* years in the host State. (Generally, a period will be continuous provided that any absences are limited to no more than six months out of every year. The right may be lost if there is a continuous absence of over two years.)

4. The right to be treated equally to nationals

i. The basic position

Once installed in a host State, Art 45(3)(c) TFEU, reiterated in Arts 1 and 2, Regulation 1612/68, provides that migrant workers must not be discriminated against on the basis of their nationality, *in terms of their employment*, remuneration and other conditions of work and employment. This is supported by other areas of the TFEU, in particular Art 18, which provides a more general right not to be discriminated against on the basis of nationality.

Articles 7 to 9, Reg 1612/68 expand upon equality in employment, providing that migrant workers should also be treated equally with nationals in *areas outside employment*, such as the provision of social advantages, access to vocational training and housing.

While discrimination on the basis of nationality is clearly outlawed, the Regulation does recognise, however, that conditions may sometimes need to be applied by reason of the nature of the post to be filled. Article 3, Reg 1612/68, in particular, recognises the need to ensure linguistic proficiency. In Case 379/87, *Groener v Minister of Education*, the Court of Justice provided some assistance in understanding how such conditions should be applied. Groener, a Dutch national, was not appointed to a teaching post at an Irish college when she failed an oral test. The test, which related to her competency in Gaelic, applied to both nationals and migrant workers alike (i.e. it was not directly discriminatory) and had been introduced to encourage the use of the language. The Court explained that such policies must not be disproportionate to the aim to be achieved by that policy, nor should the manner in which it is applied discriminate against migrant workers. The Irish rule satisfied these criteria and was held to be lawful.

Directive 2004/38 EC also takes up the theme of equal treatment, with Art 24 providing that workers should normally enjoy 'equal treatment with nationals', which supports the idea of equality *outside* employment, as well as within.

ii. The approach of the Court of Justice

The Court of Justice has, on numerous occasions, been called upon to clarify the situation with regard to equality and migrant workers, in particular the extent of the 'social advantages' to be enjoyed by migrant workers. The Court has made it clear that the term should not be interpreted restrictively.

In Case 207/78, *Ministère Public v Even* and *ONPTS*, the Court provided guidance as to the factors that should be taken into account when determining what rights amount to 'social advantages'. The case provides a test for 'social advantages' known as the *'Even Formula'*, which provides that a social advantage is a benefit not directly linked to a contract of employment but granted to workers because of their status or as a result of their residency. The Court also explained that the likelihood of the benefit accruing from the 'advantage' facilitating mobility within the EU was a relevant consideration.

An interesting, if now rather elderly, case that demonstrates the extent of 'social advantage' is Case 59/85, *Netherlands v Reed*. Here, the Court provided that an unmarried, migrant worker may enjoy the presence of his/her partner (who failed to have rights of entry and residence independently) as a 'social advantage' *provided* that, under domestic law, married and unmarried partners enjoy the same rights in that State. This approach has now been incorporated into Directive 2004/38, which provides that a 'partner with whom the Union citizen has a durable relationship' shall benefit from rights under the Directive (Art 3), although Art 2(b) of the same Directive provides that registered partnerships will *only* provide such rights for the 'partner' if the 'host Member State treats registered partnerships as equivalent to marriage'.

The right to claim equal social advantages has not been without its limitations, however, and it was once thought that social advantages were only available to persons entitled to reside by reason of employment, and not to persons, for example, permitted more temporary rights of residence. This position has now been somewhat tempered, however, as EU citizenship has provided *job seekers* with the right to claim certain social security benefits (for example, Case C-138/02, *Collins*, in which Job Seekers' Allowance was held to be a benefit which was 'intended to facilitate employment' and could not, therefore be withheld by the host State) and other benefits such as subsidised loans (Case C-209/03, *Bidar*, in which, on the basis of rights emanating from Arts 18 and 21 TFEU, it was provided that the right to a subsidised student loan could not lawfully be refused, provided the individual was 'sufficiently integrated' into the host State).

iii. Further development of the rules on 'discrimination'

Indirect discrimination

While EU rules unquestionably prohibit direct discrimination on grounds of nationality, the Court of Justice has also outlawed indirect discrimination, that is, for example, the imposition of national rules that are *more easily satisfied* by nationals than by migrant workers. This can be evidenced by Case C-237/94, *O'Flynn v Adjudication Officer*, where the Court was prepared to recognise that an apparently neutral UK rule which allowed workers to claim burial grants, but only when the burial was held in the UK, to be discriminatory and consequently contrary to Union law. (This can be compared to the manner in which both distinctly and indistinctly applicable measures may be prohibited under rules relating to the free movement of goods (Chapter 7).)

Access to the employment market

The Court of Justice has been prepared to go beyond merely prohibiting measures that *actually* discriminate – either directly or indirectly – between domestic and migrant workers, highlighting that any measure that discourages free movement may be prohibited.

In Case C-415/93, *Union Royale Belge des Sociétés de Football Association ASBL v Bosman* (the *Bosman* case), the Court explained that measures which restrict the freedom of movement of workers are prohibited *despite* not discriminating on grounds of nationality. In *Bosman*, the transnational transfer system relating to footballers was held to be an excessive obstacle to free movement, as it was capable of preventing players from obtaining employment in other Member States. However, it was also explained that such restrictive measures may be *objectively justified* by a Member State on public interest grounds.

Justification of indirect discrimination and restrictive measures

It should be noted that indirect discrimination may be subject to objective justification by the host State (Case 279/93, *Schumacker*, and Case 204/90, *Bachmann*, relating to tax rules), while direct discrimination may not.

Although first developed in relation to the free movement of services (Case 33/74, *Van Binsbergen*, and Case 279/80, *Webb*), the Court has also provided that where a national measure hinders free movement rather than discriminates against non-nationals, that measure may be justified in appropriate circumstances (*Bosman*).

In Case C-55/94, *Gebhard*, the European Court provided that 'national measures liable to hinder or make less attractive the exercise of fundamental freedoms guaranteed by the Treaty must fulfil four conditions', if they are not to fall foul of Union law. The Court went on to list the following conditions:

- the rules must be applied in a non-discriminatory manner;
- they must be justified by imperative requirements in the general interest;
- they must be suitable for securing the attainment of the objective which they pursue;
- they must not go beyond what is necessary to attain it (proportionality).

This approach can be compared to the Court's approach in relation to free movement of goods. In *Cassis*, the Court of Justice developed the 'Rule of Reason', which provides circumstances in which a restrictive measure could be justified. It can be argued that the Court's jurisprudence in both areas has developed on the basis of similar reasoning.

5. The right of migrant workers to remain after employment has ceased

Article 45(d) TFEU provides workers with the right to remain in a host State after being employed in that State.

The right of a worker to remain in a host State on retirement or where she/he ceases to be employed as a result of permanent incapacity is now expanded upon by Art 17, Directive 2004/38. While the right of permanent residence is provided, by Art 16, to all workers who have been resident for a continuous *five-year* period (discussed above), those who reach the retirement age of the host State after:

- working in that State for at least the preceding 12 months of their retirement; *and*
- having resided there continuously for at least three years;

will also enjoy the same rights of permanent residence.

Similarly, those who are permanently incapacitated, as a result of an industrial accident or occupational disease, will enjoy permanent rights of residence irrespective of how long they have resided in that State. Those who are incapacitated by other illnesses will, however, be required to have completed at least two years' continuous residence in order to be entitled to reside permanently.

6. Rights of workers who live in one State but work in another

Certain workers may find themselves working in one host State while residing in another. Providing such workers can demonstrate:

- three years' continuous residence and employment in the territory of a host State where they wish to remain; and
- that they return at least once a week to that State;

they will have the right of permanent residency in the State in which they are domiciled, after ceasing work in the second host State (Art 17, Directive 2004/38).

7. Rights and workers' families

Primary legislation does not refer to a migrant worker's right to be joined by his/her family in a host State. This has been left to secondary legislation and Directive 2004/38 now provides rights in relation to workers' families.

i. The composition of a worker's 'family'

Articles 2 and 3, Directive 2004/38 provide that a 'family member', *irrespective of nationality*, includes:

- the spouse of the worker;
- a partner with whom the worker has entered into a registered partnership, *providing* that the host State recognises such partnerships as equivalent to marriage;
- a direct descendant under 21, or dependant of the worker or his/her spouse or partner;
- a direct ascendant, provided they are dependent on the worker, spouse or partner;
- any other dependent family member, who in the 'home' State was resident in the household *or* who has serious health problems requiring personal care;
- any other family members who, in the country from where the worker has migrated, were dependants or members of the household of the worker or where serious health grounds strictly require personal care of the family member by the worker;
- a partner with whom the worker has a durable relationship.[1] (Note that it is for the host State to investigate this and to justify any denial of entry or residence.)

ii. Rights to be enjoyed by workers' families

Where family members are citizens of one of the EU Member States, both the Treaty (Art 20 TFEU) and secondary legislation (Directive 2004/38) make it clear that a general right of free movement is available to them as Union citizens.

---

1 The term 'spouse' has been restrictively interpreted by the Court to include legally married persons only (Case 59/85, *Reed*). However, in that case, the Court went on to explain that in a Member State where a stable relationship enjoyed by an unmarried couple is accorded similar status to marriage, this will be considered to be a 'social advantage', as to treat such couples differently would amount to discrimination. It would appear that this interpretation of the legislation has now been incorporated into the new directive by virtue of Art 3, Directive 2004/38.

In addition, family members who are nationals of countries outside the EU also have rights of free movement, albeit indirect, as a result of their relationship with the worker. As already touched on above, it is important to understand that the EU citizen must first have exercised their right of free movement *before* their family members may enjoy free movement rights (Case C-127/08, *Metock*).

Family rights of exit, entry and residence

Directive 2004/39 provides that family members who are EU citizens enjoy the same rights of exit and entry as the worker. Where a family member is not an EU citizen, again rights are very similar, other than that they may be required to provide an entry visa or valid residence card (Art 5, Directive 2004/38).

As mentioned above, all Union citizens have a right of residence in a host State for up to three months. This right is also extended to family members who are non-EU citizens, if accompanying the worker (Art 6, Directive 2004/38).

Similarly, family members, irrespective of their nationality and by virtue of their relationship to the worker, will be afforded the right of residence for more than three months on the same basis as the worker (Art 7). In the case of non-EU citizens, this is subject to the issue of a residence card, which should be issued expediently by the host State, on production of certain documentation (listed in Art 10, Directive 2004/38).

Once family members have been legally resident in the host State for a continuous period of five years, they will, under the same conditions as the worker, have the right of permanent residence in the host State (Arts 16 and 17, Art 18 for non-EU nationals, Directive 2004/38).

Families and the right to take up employment

If the family member is an EU citizen, the right to take up employment is provided by Art 45 TFEU. Taking up employment in a host State will, of course, give the family member independent rights and, consequently, they will no longer need to depend on rights provided through their relationship with the original worker.

Article 23, Directive 2004/38, reiterates this and also extends the right to non-EU family members who have rights of residence.

Families and the right to education

Under Art 12, Reg 1612/68, children of a worker residing in a host State enjoy non-discriminatory access to general educational, apprenticeship and vocational training schemes. This has been broadly interpreted by the Court of Justice, which has held that the children of migrant workers are entitled to exactly the same benefits as children of domestic workers, including educational grants (Case 76/72, *Michel S*), and it would appear that the exception to this – contained in Art 24, Directive 2004/38 – has been interpreted by the Court of Justice in a manner which appears to have negated it (Case C-209/03, *R v London Borough of Ealing and Secretary of State for Education and Skills, ex p Bidar*, where, Bidar, a French national resident with his grandmother in the UK, failed to meet the residence requirement of three years in order to obtain a grant. It was argued that, as an EU citizen, he should be entitled to a grant on the same terms as UK citizens, a proposition with which the Court of Justice agreed).

The broad interpretative approach of the Court can also be evidenced by decisions such as Cases 389 and 390/87, *Echternach* and *Moritz v Netherlands Ministry for Education and Science*, where the Court held that children of migrant workers could remain in the host State to finish their education, even when their parents had returned home. Similarly, in Case C-7/94, *Gaal*, the Court provided that educational rights include the right to complete a course, even after a once dependent child reaches the age of 21, as to act otherwise would discourage integration.

It is not clear whether workers' spouses/partners enjoy such wide rights in relation to education, but they have been held to be entitled to equal access to educational, apprenticeship or vocational training schemes by reason of non-discrimination provisions enshrined in Art 18 TFEU (for example, Case 152/82, *Forcheri v Belgium*). Such rights would now appear to have been further strengthened by the requirement in Art 24, Directive 2004/38 that workers and their family members, whether EU nationals or not, should be treated equally with nationals.

Families and the right to remain: death or divorce

Directive 2004/38 not only details the rights of workers to remain in a host State, but also provides that the residence rights of a worker's family will normally remain unchanged should the worker die or leave the host State, although the right to remain of family members who are non-EU citizens will be reliant on their having resided with the worker, in the host State, for at least 12 months prior to the worker's death (Art 12 of the Directive). The

Court of Justice has also confirmed that the surviving family of a deceased worker will enjoy equality of treatment with nationals of that State (Case 32/75, *Cristini v SNCF*).

Divorce, annulment or termination of a registered partnership should also not affect the right of family members to reside (Art 13, Directive 2004/38), although conditions relating to the length of the relationship, custody of children and so on, may apply where the spouse/partner is a non-EU citizen.

Other rights relating to family members

As has already been established, the rights afforded to workers' families often flow from their relationship with a migrant worker. It should also be remembered that Art 18 TFEU provides *all* EU citizens with a general right not to be discriminated against on grounds of their nationality, while Art 24, Directive 2204/38 extends this right to family members who are non-EU citizens.

More specifically, the Court of Justice has elaborated on the extent of dependant rights in a number of cases, particularly with regard to 'social advantages'. In Case 32/75, *Cristini v SNCF*, the Court held that the right 'cannot be interpreted restrictively', as to do so would hamper integration.

III. FREE MOVEMENT: LIMITATIONS ON WORKERS' RIGHTS

1. Restrictions on exit, entry and residence on grounds of public policy, public security and public health

The EU recognises that there are certain circumstances under which it is neither reasonable nor desirable to allow workers – *or their families* – the right to move freely within the EU. Union law therefore provides that Member States may deny rights in certain circumstances.

Article 45(3) TFEU provides that States may deny workers the right of free movement on the grounds of public policy, public security or public health.

i. Secondary legislation and the limitation of rights

The derogation provided by Art 45(3) TFEU is repeated, and expanded upon, by Art 27, Directive 2004/38. The Directive provides that measures taken on the basis of public security, public policy or public health must not be invoked to serve economic ends.

Measures taken on grounds of public policy or security must also comply with the principle of proportionality and be based exclusively on the *personal conduct* of the individual concerned. It is also provided that the existence of previous criminal convictions will not *automatically* allow a Member State to deny a worker his rights of entry and residence.

The Directive further provides that the personal conduct of the individual concerned must present a (1) *genuine*, (2) *present* and (3) *sufficiently serious threat*, affecting one of the fundamental interests of the State, while it is prescribed that prohibitions which are *general* in nature shall not be accepted.

In order to ascertain whether an individual presents such a threat, certain procedures apply. When issuing a registration certificate or residence card or, in the absence of a registration system, no later than three months after the entry of the individual into a host State, a host State *may* request that the home State provide information relating to the previous police record of the individual. A home State is required to provide an answer within two months.

Should a host State expel an individual on grounds of public policy, public security or public health, the home State which issued the passport of the individual concerned must allow the individual to re-enter its territory.

ii. Procedural safeguards

Article 28, Directive 2004/38, provides what considerations a host State should take into account before taking the decision to expel. These include:

- length of residence in the host State;
- age;
- health;
- family;
- economic situation;
- social and cultural integration into the host State;
- links with country of origin.

It is also provided that, where the individual has a right of permanent residence in a host State, the decision to expel should only be taken on *serious* grounds of public policy and/or security. Where the individual is an EU citizen who has:

- resided in the host State for 10 years; or
- is a minor (unless in the best interests of the child);

the decision to expel should only be taken on *imperative* grounds of public security.

In addition, the Directive provides that any decision to expel must normally be provided in full and in writing (Art 30) and that there must be an appeal process in place (Art 31). Those excluded may also submit an application to have the expulsion order lifted, after a reasonable period, which should be no longer than five years (Art 32).

iii. The approach of the Court of Justice to restrictions on exit, entry and residence

The Court has taken a narrow approach to the interpretation of the legislation restricting the free movement of workers. As with the exceptions to the rules governing free movement of goods (Art 36 TFEU), exceptions to the free movement of workers must be proportionate and objectively justifiable. The case law outlined below precedes Directive 2004/38 but is likely to still be relevant, as it can be seen that the decisions of the Court of Justice have now been largely incorporated into secondary legislation.

- In Case 36/75, *Rutili v Ministre de l'Interieur*, the Court provided that a Member State claiming derogation on the grounds of public policy and/or security may only deny a worker his rights if his presence constitutes a 'genuine and sufficiently serious threat to public policy'.
- This was extended in Case 30/77, *R v Bouchereau*, where the Court provided that the threat must also 'affect one of the fundamental interests of the State'.
- In Cases 115 and 116/81, *Adoui* and *Cornuaille v Belgian State* (the *French Prostitutes* case), the Court of Justice held that derogation on grounds of public policy does not allow expulsion of a migrant worker where similar conduct by a national would not incur a proportionately restrictive sanction. (In *Adoui*, French nationals were denied entry to Belgium due to their 'moral standards', despite the fact that prostitution is not illegal there – an obvious example of discrimination against migrants.)

It is obvious that the dicta of the Court run in parallel to secondary legislation by providing that criminal convictions do not provide grounds for exclusion *unless* they provide evidence of a present threat, as can be demonstrated by the following cases:

- Case 30/77, *R v Bouchereau*, where B, a French national, came to work in the United Kingdom in 1975. He was convicted of unlawful possession of drugs in June 1976, having pleaded guilty to a similar offence in January 1976 (for which he received a 12-month conditional discharge). The magistrates' court made a reference to the Court of Justice, questioning the extent to which previous convictions may be considered as a ground for exclusion. The Court held that previous criminal convictions may only be taken into account as evidence of personal conduct where it constitutes a present threat to the requirements of public policy, by indicating a likelihood of recurrence. Past conduct alone may, however, be sufficient to constitute a present threat if the conduct can be considered to be sufficiently serious.

- Case 67/74, *Bonsignore v Oberstadtdirektor of the City of Cologne*, in which B, an Italian working in Germany, accidentally shot his brother. He was convicted of unlawful possession of a firearm and was ordered to be deported. He challenged the deportation order and the German courts made a reference to the Court of Justice, questioning whether deportation may be justified on public policy grounds as a general preventative measure to deter others. The Court held that the public policy requirement may only be invoked to justify a deportation for breaches of the peace and public security which may be committed by the individual concerned and not for reasons of a general preventative nature.

iv. The 'public health' limitation

As touched on above, Article 45(3) TFEU also provides that the Member States may deny workers the right of free movement on grounds of public health.

Article 29, Directive 2004/38, expands upon this by outlining the diseases for which expulsion is allowed but also providing that diseases which occur after three months of entry into a host State will not constitute grounds for expulsion.

2. Restrictions on 'employment in the public service'

Article 45(3) TFEU provides that the provisions of Art 45 'shall not apply to employment in the public service'. This means that a worker may be prevented from taking up a job in the 'public sector' of the host State: it does not, however, extend to the limitation of rights of entry, etc.

The exact scope of 'public service' is not defined by legislation and, not surprisingly as it provides an exception to the fundamental EU principle of free movement, the concept has been narrowly interpreted by the Court of Justice. The Court has shed light on the extent and application of the rule and the following cases are particularly enlightening.

First, the Court has held that Art 45(4) TFEU cannot be invoked by Member States in relation to the terms and conditions of employment as it applies only to *access* to employment (Case 152/73, *Sotgui v Deutsche Bundespost*).

In Case 149/79, *Commission v Belgium* (*Re Public Employees*), Belgian law reserving all posts in the public service for Belgian nationals, irrespective of the duties performed, was found to come outside the scope of the Art 45(4) TFEU. To come within the ambit of Art 45(4), the Court held that employment must involve 'direct or indirect participation in the exercise of powers conferred by public law and duties designed to safeguard the general interests of the State or other public authorities'. While it is self-evident that higher-level posts are the most likely to come within the scope of Art 45, lower-level posts – with, for example, access to 'sensitive' information, such as cleaners and night-watchmen – *may* also be included.

The implication of this and other supporting decisions is that posts in which the post-holder owes a particular allegiance to the State may be included (e.g. the armed forces, police, judiciary, tax authorities and high-ranking civil servants, etc.). This view is reinforced by the Notice in 1988 (OJ No 72/2), in which the Commission provided some guidance as to which post would be covered. The Commission concluded that the following would be unlikely to be covered:

- public health services;
- teaching in State educational establishments;
- research for non-military purposes in public establishments;
- public bodies responsible for administering commercial services.

In view of the Court's restrictive attitude and Commission guidance, this has remained a contentious area. While the EU recognises a need for Member States to preserve their own national identity, the Union has not been prepared to allow them to do this to the detriment of free movement.

IV. ENFORCING WORKERS' RIGHTS TO FREE MOVEMENT

In addition to understanding that EU law provides individuals with rights in relation to free movement throughout the EU, it is also necessary to consider how such rights may be enforced and against whom.

Under the doctrine of direct effect, individuals may normally enforce their EU law rights before national courts. The Court of Justice has been particularly concerned to emphasise that Art 45 TFEU provides rights to individuals and, in Case 167/73, *Commission v France* (the *French Seamen* case), held that Art 45 is 'directly applicable in the legal system of every Member State'. In addition, the Court provided that all conflicting national law should be rendered inapplicable.

Furthermore, the Court has also made it clear that the Treaty Article not only places obligations on Member States, but also places a duty on individuals to do likewise. In *Bosman*, for example, the defendants in the action were, amongst others, the Belgium Football Association, while in Case C-282/98, *Roman Angonese v Cassa di Risparmio di Bolzana Spa*, the Court of Justice specifically explained that the Union principle of free movement of workers places obligations not only on public bodies but also on *private* persons (in this case a bank). This means that Art 45 is horizontally directly effective. Enforcing rights emanating from a directive is, of course, a different matter, and rights contained in Directive 2004/38 should have been made available through national implementing legislation.

In addition, should a Member State fail to comply with its obligations in relation to the free movement, the Commission (or second Member State) may initiate enforcement proceedings against that State (Arts 258–260 TFEU, discussed in Chapter 6), while a sufficiently serious breach by a Member State failure could result in an action for damages against the State (State Liability/Damages, Chapter 5).

V. FREE MOVEMENT AND THE RIGHTS OF 'NON-ECONOMICALLY ACTIVE' CITIZENS

It is understandable that the original EEC Treaty was silent on the rights to free movement of those who were not economically active, as the activities of the EU have been traditionally economic in nature. However, the signal for change was the introduction of three Directives (often known as the '90s Directives') which were enacted in the 1990s to provide non-economically active EU nationals – namely students, retirees (either through age or ill-health) and those with sufficient resources not to become a burden on the social security system of the host State – with rights of free movement and residence *comparable, but not identical*, to those enjoyed by workers and other economically active groups. The introduction of EU citizenship by the 1992 Maastricht Treaty (TEU), with its corresponding 'right to move and reside freely within the territory of the Member States' (now Art 21 TFEU) was a further signal that rights of free movement were to be extended.

As already touched upon in regard to workers' rights, in April 2006 new legislation, in the form of Directive 2004/38 on Citizens Rights of Free Movement, on the rights of EU citizens and their families to move and reside freely within the EU, was introduced. It repealed earlier secondary legislation, including the '90s Directives', and it is this Directive which now largely provides the detailed rules by which non-economically active Union citizens may move to, and stay in, a host State. Briefly, such rights relate to:

- *The right of exit from a home State (Art 4, Directive 2004/38) and entry into the host State (Art 5, Directive 2004/38)*: Rights contained in these Articles relate largely to the formalities and documentation required, in order to ensure that a home or host State cannot create a barrier to free movement by imposing unnecessary formality.

- *The right of residence (Arts 6–15, Directive 2004/38)*: Providing that an EU citizen has a valid ID card or passport, Art 6 Directive 2004/38 provides a right of temporary residence for up to three months for citizens and their families (including non-EU family members).

- *Extension of the right of residence*: Provided under Art 7, Directive 2004/38, citizens and their families who can demonstrate that they have sufficient resources not to become a financial burden on the host State, including health insurance, will have extended rights of residence. Articles 8 to 11, Directive 2004/38 specify the administrative formalities that need to be satisfied, while Arts 12 to 14, Directive 2004/38 relate to continuing rights of family members should the relevant EU citizen die, leave the host State or divorce their spouse. Article 15, Directive 2004/38 refers to the procedural safeguards put in place to ensure that their rights are not denied.

- *Rights of permanent residence (Art 16, Directive 2004/38)*: The Directive provides the general rule that where EU citizens and their family members have lawfully resided in a host State for a continuous period of five years, they will have the right of permanent residence, although this right can be lost following an individual's absence from the host State for a period of two or more years. Once more, rights are subject to administrative formalities as set out in Chapters IV and V of Directive 2004/38.

• *What amounts to a family member?* As already highlighted above, EU citizens have the right to be accompanied by family members and Arts 2 and 3, Directive 2004/38 provide a comprehensive list of those to be considered 'family members'. (In Case C- 200/02, *Zhu and Chen v Sec of State for Home Dept*, the Court of Justice developed its interpretation of family member and held that where the citizen in question is a minor, a non-EU primary carer of the child must be allowed to reside with the child in the host State.)

1. EU citizens and the right to equal treatment with nationals

Citizens' rights to equal treatment on the basis of nationality is an area of EU law which has developed considerably since Union citizenship was first introduced. Article 18 TFEU prohibits discrimination on the basis of nationality in general terms, while Art 24, Directive 2004/38 makes it clear that citizens and their families who have exercised their right to free movement shall enjoy equal treatment with nationals of the host State. Such rights are limited, however, in terms of any financial assistance which may be available, as Art 24(2) of the Directive also provides that Member States are *not* obliged to award job seekers or students equality in regard to such financial assistance, unless they have rights of permanent residency. Further, in Case C-413/99, *Baumbast*, the Court of Justice confirmed that Art 21 TFEU has direct effect, emphasising that any limitations applied by the Member States on the free movement of citizens are subject to the principle of proportionality.

While it had been *originally* assumed that the right to enjoy social advantages on the same basis as nationals was limited to those who were economically active, cases such as Case C-85/96, *Martinez Sala*, and Case C-184/99, *Grzelczyk*, have clarified that *all* citizens enjoy such rights under Art 18 TFEU. However, the *Grzelczyk* decision also made it clear that Art 24(2) of the Directive, which allows Member States to limit entitlement to social assistance during the first three months of residence, still applies.

More recent case law has continued to focus on the rights of (non-economically active) EU citizens. For example, the cases of *Bidar* and *Forster* (Case C-209/03, *Bidar*, Case C158/07, *Forster*) involved students who had had applications for financial support turned down by the host State. The Court of Justice emphasised that migrant students are able to rely on Art 18 TFEU, although it is not unreasonable for the host State to require a certain level of integration to be demonstrated by the student, such as residence in the host State for a certain period of time, before financial support is made available. The Court made it clear that Art 18 TFEU must be read in conjunction with the provisions on EU citizenship and has cautioned Member States against the application of conditions which are liable to deter citizens from making use of their rights to free movement (Joined Cases C-11/06 and C-12/06, *Morgan, Iris Butcher*).

Similarly, in regard to job seekers' rights in regard to social security benefits, the Court of Justice has made it clear that it is no longer possible for a host State to routinely deny citizens benefits of a financial nature which are intended to facilitate access to employment, such as Job Seekers' Allowance unless objectively justifiable for reasons unrelated to nationality (Case C-138/02, *Collins*, Case C258/04, *Ioannidis*).

Workers' rights:
– **Art 45 TFEU** provides the right to take up employment on the same basis as nationals of the host State. Workers also given the right to remain when employment ceases
– **Reg 1612/68** sets out further rules on eligibility for employment, equality & family rights
– **Dir 2004/38** expands rights, including equal treatment outside employment (social advantages), the right to be accompanied by family members
– **Dir 2004/38** also provides administrative detail in regard to entry, exit & residence

Limiting workers' rights:
– **Art 45** provides that MSs may deny workers rights of free movement on grounds of public policy, security & health
– **Art 45** also provides that workers' right to take up public-sector employment may be limited by State
– **Dir 2004/38** provides additional detail in regard to limitation of workers' rights and expulsion, including procedural safeguards

The status of 'worker':
Term is defined by the Court of Justice. Workers must demonstrate that they undertake genuine work of an economic nature (*Levin*).

Citizens' & Workers' Rights to Free Movement within the EU

Job seekers and students:
Citizenship of EU provides non-economically active citizens with limited rights to free movement to seek employment and study, provided they do not place a burden on the host State (**Art 20 TFEU & Dir 2004/38**)

Non-economically active EU citizens:
– All EU citizens have the right to free movement for up to 3 months (**Dir 2004/38**)
– Further right to reside dependent on not being a financial burden on the host State
– Citizens' right to equality increasingly developed by Court of Justice

Workers' families:
– Family members (as set out in **Dir 2004/38**) given right to accompany worker (includes non-EU citizens) and reside
– Family members enjoy equal rights with nationals, including social advantages, right to remain, etc.

In a nutshell, in the *Morgan* case, the Court provides that such restrictions can now only be justified in the light of Union law if 'based on objective considerations of public interest independent of the nationality of the persons concerned and if it is proportionate to the legitimate objective pursued by the provisions of national law . . .'

VI. FREEDOM OF ESTABLISHMENT AND THE PROVISION OF SERVICES

In addition to promoting the free movement of workers and their families within the EU, the Treaty also provides similar rights to the self-employed, businesses wishing to establish themselves in a host Member State and also those wishing to provide a service in a host State.

Articles 49 to 55 TFEU prohibit discriminatory restrictions from being placed on those who wish to establish a business in a host State, while Arts 56 to 62 TFEU afford the right of free movement to those who wish to provide a service in a host State, normally without being based there.

While the Treaty provides three sets of provisions covering the free movement of the three different 'groups', the Court has emphasised that much common ground exists between them. In Case 48/75, *Royer*, for example, the Court observed that the free movement of workers, freedom of establishment and freedom to provide services are all 'based on the same principles in so far as they concern the entry into and the residence in the territory of Member States of persons covered by Community law and the prohibition of all discrimination between them on grounds of nationality'.

It should be borne in mind, however, that while the *principles* behind the various provisions have much in common, the *rules* applying to artificial legal persons can be quite different. In view of the constraints of this text, both right of establishment and provision of services are provided in outline only.

1. Right of establishment (Arts 49 to 55 TFEU)

Article 49 TFEU provides EU citizens with the right to establish a business (that is, set up a permanent base) in a host State under the same conditions as those enjoyed by nationals of that State.

This right is also applicable to the setting up of agencies, branches or subsidiaries of companies or firms that have already been established in another State. (Article 54 TFEU specifically provides that such businesses must be treated in the same way as natural persons.)

Those carrying out the activities set out above are required to comply with the national laws applicable in the host State *unless* those laws can be shown to discriminate on the basis of nationality. Such discrimination is prohibited both by Art 49 TFEU and, in a more general manner, by Art 18 TFEU. Discriminatory rules will be seen as conflicting with Union law and must consequently be set aside.

Just as Art 45 TFEU provides the framework for the free movement of workers, so Art 49 TFEU provides a framework for rights of establishment. Once more, the relevant primary legislation is supported and expanded upon by secondary legislation and decisions of the Court of Justice. In particular, it may be worth mentioning Directive 2006/123 which, although relating to service provision, contains principles common to both services and establishment. As the final date for transposition of the Directive was 28 December 2009, it is yet to be seen exactly what influence it may have on issues relating to establishment.

i. What amounts to 'establishment'?

The Court of Justice has defined establishment as 'the actual pursuit of an economic activity through a fixed establishment in another Member State for an indefinite period' (Case C-221/89, *Factortame*).

ii. Natural legal persons

In some situations there may be initial confusion over whether someone is employed or self-employed. The Court, however, has made it clear that anyone who is working under the control of another and is receiving a wage or salary will be considered a worker, while those involved in the setting up and running of a business for themselves, rather than on behalf of another, will be considered to be self-employed (Case C-456/02 *Trojani v Centre public d'aide sociale*).

iii. Artificial legal persons

As touched on above, in addition to natural legal persons who wish to establish themselves in a host State, artificial legal persons are also afforded rights of establishment. (Article 54 TFEU should be read here, as it provides a list of artificial persons who may benefit from rules on establishment.)

To enjoy such rights, companies must demonstrate that they are already legally established in one Member State, often known as the 'primary State', and wish to conduct business in a second Member State, or 'secondary State' (Art 54 TFEU).

This has, on occasion, been problematic, as companies registered in one State and established in a second State have then moved their main place of business to the second State in order to benefit, for example, from a more lax regulatory regime (as in Case 81/87, *R v HM Treasury ex p Daily Mail* or where the business was able to avoid onerous taxation rules in its 'home' State). The Court of Justice has since provided that only the *primary* State can raise objections to such behaviour (Case C-212/97, *Centros*).

iv. Rights of the self-employed and their families: exit, entry and residence

Article 7, Directive 2004/38, is quite specific in that it provides rights not only for workers and their families but also self-employed persons and their families. Consequently, the rights outlined above, in relation to exit, entry and residence, will apply in the same manner to the self-employed and their families as they do to workers and their families and so therefore need not be reiterated here.

As the Court of Justice has also provided that the rules relating to workers and the self-employed are based on the same principles (*Royer*), it can safely be assumed that an analogous approach should be taken in regard to their interpretation and application.

v. Equality: what amounts to 'discrimination'?

In line with its case law in the area of free movement of workers – and free movement of goods – the Court of Justice has provided that both directly and indirectly discriminatory rules may breach Art 49 TFEU.

While national rules which apply to non-nationals *only* will be *prima facie* discriminatory, national laws which appear to apply equally to non-nationals and nationals alike may also breach Art 49 TFEU (Case 71/76, *Thieffry*). In Case 143/87, *Stanton v INASTI*, the Court went further by providing that any national rule, whether discriminatory or not, which 'might place Community citizens at a disadvantage' will be prohibited *unless* it can be objectively justified by the State wishing to apply it.

The question of whether 'reverse discrimination' is prohibited by Art 49 TFEU has also been considered by the Court of Justice. Reverse discrimination occurs when the discrimination complained of takes place within the national's *home* State. An illustration of this can be found in Case

115/78, *Knoors v Secretary of State for Economic Affairs,* where qualifications obtained by Mr Knoors, a Dutch national, while resident in Belgium were not recognised by the Dutch State when he returned home to Holland.

It is now clear that any rule which discourages free movement of goods, persons or services is likely to be prohibited by Union law – unless it is indirectly discriminatory, in which case it may be objectively justified. (The issue of 'justification' is set out above under the heading of 'The public interest justification', which lists the conditions that must be fulfilled if a rule is not to fall foul of Union law, as provided by the Court in the case of *Gebhard.*)

vi. Recognition of qualifications

National rules relating to qualifications can result in a significant barrier to the free movement of persons. An example of this can be found with regard to solicitors in England and Wales, whose qualifications must comply with rules set by the Solicitors Regulation Authority. Failure to comply with such rules will result in an individual being prohibited from carrying out his/her profession.

Under Art 53 TFEU, the Council is provided with the authority to issue directives in regard to recognition of training and qualifications obtained within the Union and, as a result, a considerable amount of harmonising legislation has been enacted. (You may want to visit the Europa website to research this in more detail. Directives 77/249/EEC and 98/5/EC, for example, relate specifically to legal qualifications.) Not all professions are covered in this way and in the absence of such legislation, the Court of Justice has held that national authorities have an obligation to consider the training and/or qualifications held by a non-national and compare them to the domestic provision/requirements. Where they are found to be equivalent, the host State must recognise them as such (Case 340/89, *Vlassopoulou*).

If they are found not to be equivalent, the host State must provide reasons for its decision, which must be open to judicial review (Case 222/86, *UNECTEF v Heylens*). If qualifications are found to be 'part equivalent', a host State may require further training to be undertaken in order to 'make up the difference'.

vii. Limitations on freedom of establishment

As we have already seen in relation to workers, restrictive and/or discriminatory measures may be justified on grounds of public policy, security and health and also with regard to employment in the public sector. Similar grounds may also be argued in relation to establishment (and the provision of services).

viii. Limitation on grounds of 'public policy, public service and public health'

Article 53 TFEU provides for limitation of rights 'on grounds of public policy, public security or public health'. The Court has held that these grounds should be applied in a similar manner to those found under Art 45(3) TFEU (Case 36/74, *Walrave and Koch*) and, indeed, the secondary legislation expanding upon this derogation specifically relates to both workers and establishment (Directive 2004/38).

ix. The exercise of 'official authority' limitation

Article 51 TFEU provides that rights concerning establishment may not be available to those who 'exercise official authority'.

This exception will be relevant in relation to the exercise of an official (State) power. The Court of Justice has confirmed that it is to be applied in a similar manner to the exception found under Art 45(4) TFEU, that is, the 'employment in the public service' exception to free movement of workers (Case 2/74, *Reyners v Belgium*). As the Court has interpreted the 'public service' exception narrowly with regard to Art 45 (4), a similar approach can safely be assumed here.

x. Enforcing rights of establishment

Case 2/74, *Reyners*, provides authority that Art 49 TFEU is directly effective.

In Case 36/74, *Walrave and Koch*, which related to the rights of the self-employed, the Court appeared to extend the scope of the legislation beyond merely the actions of public authorities. In view of the decisions of the Court in *Bosman* and *Angonese* (discussed above in regard to workers) and the analogous approach of the Court in all areas relating to free movement, it is likely that Art 49 TFEU is at least partly horizontally directly effective, although there has yet to be a totally decisive judgment.

2. Free movement and the provision of services (Arts 56 to 62 TFEU)

While rights of establishment relate to rights enjoyed by EU citizens who wish to set up a permanent base in a host State (that is, for an unspecified period), rights of free movement to provide services normally relate to the carrying out of an economic activity for a *temporary* period, where the provider has no permanent base in that State.

The distinction may be difficult to draw on occasion – for example, in *Gebhard*, it was ruled that a service provider may have an office or other base in the host State from which he provides his (temporary) service(s). However, in that case the Court of Justice also provided that 'the temporary nature of the activities in question has to be determined in the light not only of the duration of the provision of the service, but also of its regularity, periodicity or continuity'.

Article 56 TFEU has also been held to prohibit measures that restrict the provision of services, where the *recipient* moves to a host State to obtain a service (Joined Cases 286/82 and 26/83, *Luisi* and *Carbone*, and Case 186/87, *Cowan v Tresor Public*). It also appears to cover situations where the service moves but neither provider nor recipient move (e.g. internet-provided services), *or* where both parties move to a third State – what is important is that there is an inter-State element to the transaction. As touched on above, Directive 2006/123 on services in the internal market has now come into force. The Directive is residual, in that it only applies where no other EU legislative act applies and as yet it still remains to be seen what the impact of the new Directive will be.

i. What is a 'service'?

Article 57 TFEU provides that to be considered a 'service', the service must be 'provided for remuneration' (which has been supported by the Court of Justice in Case 52/79, *Debauve*, where the Court made it clear that services provided gratuitously are not included). The Article also provides examples, such as activities of an industrial or commercial nature, of craftsmen and of the professions.

The Court has interpreted 'services' widely to include medical services, vocational training and tourism, and is likely to include any (lawful) temporary presence in a host State, *unless* specifically covered by another area of the Treaty.

ii. Rights of service providers

Rights of exit and entry

Rights include the right to exit a home State and enter a host State in very much the same way as provided to workers and the self-employed, as discussed above. However, as those wishing to provide – or receive – a service do not wish to establish a permanent base in a host State, rights do not include residence rights for either the provider or receiver of a service, nor normally his/her family.

Protection from discrimination

Article 56 TFEU requires the elimination of all discrimination based on nationality, against non-national providers (or receivers) of services. This Article is supported by the more general Art 18 TFEU, which requires the elimination of discrimination based on nationality.

Once more, the elimination of such discrimination has been extended to national measures which impede free movement, without necessarily *directly* discriminating (Case C-384/93, *Alpine Investments*). Again, where the national rule is not directly discriminatory, it may be objectively justified (in Cases C-369 and C-376/96, *Arblade*, the principles developed in *Gebhard* – discussed above – were once more applied).

iii. Exceptions to the right of free movement to provide services

Member States may derogate from their obligations to provide rights of free movement of services on similar grounds to those already considered in terms of workers and establishment. As has already been discussed, in regard to workers and establishment, exceptions to the right of free movement have been interpreted restrictively by the Court, thus ensuring that restrictions on free movement are kept to a minimum. Unsurprisingly, as all 'four freedoms' are intended to support the creation of a single market, the Court's approach here mirrors its approach in relation to free movement of workers and rights of establishment – and also, to a certain extent, free movement of goods (discussed in Chapter 7).

iv. Public policy, public security or public health

Article 62 TFEU specifically provides that the derogations, relating to establishment, found in Art 51 to 54 TFEU will also apply to the right to move freely to provide a service. Consequently, discussion provided above in relation to such derogations will be relevant to consider in relation to services.

v. Exercise of official authority

Article 62 TFEU also provides that the derogation relating to the exercise of official authority found in Art 51 TFEU will apply in the same manner to services.

vi. Enforcing rights to provide and receive services

Case 33/74, *Van Binsbergen*, provides authority that Art 56 TFEU has direct effect.

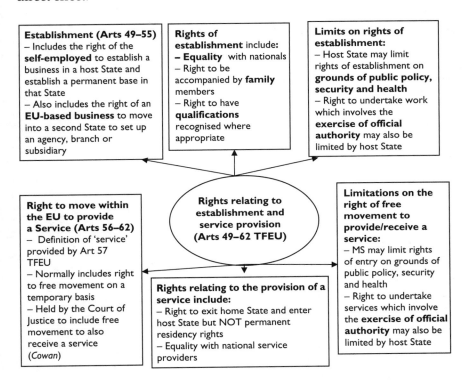

Establishment (Arts 49–55)
– Includes the right of the **self-employed** to establish a business in a host State and establish a permanent base in that State
– Also includes the right of an **EU-based business** to move into a second State to set up an agency, branch or subsidiary

Rights of establishment include:
– **Equality** with nationals
– Right to be accompanied by **family** members
– Right to have **qualifications** recognised where appropriate

Limits on rights of establishment:
– Host State may limit rights of establishment on **grounds of public policy, security and health**
– Right to undertake work which involves the **exercise of official authority** may also be limited by host State

Right to move within the EU to provide a Service (Arts 56–62)
– Definition of 'service' provided by Art 57 TFEU
– Normally includes right to free movement on a temporary basis
– Held by the Court of Justice to include free movement to also receive a service (*Cowan*)

Rights relating to establishment and service provision (Arts 49–62 TFEU)

Limitations on the right of free movement to provide/receive a service:
– MS may limit rights of entry on grounds of public policy, security and health
– Right to undertake services which involve the **exercise of official authority** may also be limited by host State

Rights relating to the provision of a service include:
– Right to exit home State and enter host State but NOT permanent residency rights
– Equality with national service providers

SOME ISSUES TO THINK ABOUT FURTHER:

- How are workers distinguishable from the self-employed and service providers?
- In outline, consider what rights are enjoyed by workers? Can, or how may, these rights be limited by Member States? Can rights relating to free movement of workers be enforced against private individuals?
- What are the main differences between the rights of workers and the rights of non-economically active EU citizens?

9 Revision and Exams

This book is not intended to be a revision workbook or a guide on how to pass exams but, *very* briefly, some hopefully helpful tips are provided below.

I. REVISION

Obvious though it may seem, ensure that you are familiar with the syllabus of your course. Always plan your revision well in advance, ensuring that you start early enough to complete it and have time for relaxation! Drawing up a revision timetable, which clearly demonstrates that you DO have enough time to complete your revision, can be invaluable in calming pre-assessment nerves.

Trying to 'learn' European law by rote is boring, hard work and unlikely to produce good results. Although some 'learning' is inevitable (legal authorities are an example), what you should do is try to ensure that you *understand* the law, particularly *why* it has developed as it has. This is because success at this level is rarely based on knowledge alone and assessment will require you to also demonstrate an ability to analyse, evaluate and apply the law if you are to achieve the best marks.

If you have worked consistently throughout your course, you should have few worries. All you will need to do is ensure that what you have learned throughout the academic year is brought back to the forefront of your memory. One of the most important things to do is to discover what you *do* know and what areas need a little more work – there is little point in spending excessive time on areas that you are sufficiently familiar with! One of the best ways of testing your knowledge is to obtain past papers, old tutorial questions or even pick out appropriate questions from a revision workbook. Sit down and attempt to answer the questions – preferably in full and under similar constraints as will be imposed in the examination room. Check your answers against your notes or textbook and this should tell you which are your weak areas, allowing you the opportunity to concentrate the majority of your revision time on these. (Do remember that revision is a skill: it needs thought and practice, just like other skills.)

As touched upon above, there is little point in sitting down with your notes or textbook and trying to learn by rote. It is far more productive to read as widely as time allows around the areas that you are finding difficult, perhaps making your own notes, and then attempt to answer further questions, once more, under examination conditions.

If you make your own notes, which is always a good idea as it aids memory, make sure that they are not too detailed. If they are, it probably indicates a lack of understanding and you may also find that there is little advantage in consulting them over a textbook. Briefer notes also tend to be the most helpful for last minute revision! You may also find it useful to use 'spider diagrams' or flowcharts, which can also be useful when constructing answer plans. Brainstorming is another useful way to 'encourage' your memory – don't discount it without giving it a try!

II. EXAMINATION TECHNIQUE

Success in examinations cannot be entirely put down to good (or bad) exam technique. Without an appropriate level of knowledge and understanding, of course, it is unlikely that exam success will be enjoyed, but good exam technique can make the difference between achieving or just missing a grade.

Exam questions will either be 'essay type' or 'problem type'. While students often profess to only being able to 'cope' with one type or the other, there is actually very little difference in what is required in terms of knowledge and understanding and both should be approached in basically the same manner.

First, always ensure that you spend an adequate amount of time carefully analysing the question. Then prepare an answer plan. You may feel that there is little time for such luxuries in a time-constrained assessment but, in reality, you will probably save time – unplanned answers often ramble and points may be repeated or irrelevant issues discussed. Your plan need not be long or complex; often a few key words, placed in an appropriate order, will be sufficient. In addition, too many answers take the 'say all you know' approach rather than targeting the specific question set and consequently don't earn the marks that your knowledge may deserve.

All answers should normally have an introduction, a 'main' part or parts, and a conclusion. A brief – *never* rambling – introduction can be seen as an opportunity to 'set the scene', provide relevant background information and/or demonstrate an understanding of how the subject matter of your answer relates to the wider view of Europe. Alternatively, if you find this difficult, an introduction can be used to briefly explain to the reader what needs to be discussed – and why – in order to answer the question. This is something that you can think about at the revision stage – but remember that if you are short of time an introduction can be seen as an unnecessary luxury.

The 'main' part of your answer should contain the 'meat': the law and its application or evaluation. When planning your answer, you should not only decide what you need to say, but also the order in which it is most effectively said. This will ensure that your answer flows logically.

The exam question will require that you reach a conclusion that actually answers the question set. Never forget to do this. You may have been asked to advise someone, consider a proposition or comment on the development of law, for example. To ensure that you have actually answered the question asked, *and not the one you would like to have been asked*, always re-read the question before embarking on your conclusion. If you discover that you have wandered from the point or missed an important point, you will then still have the opportunity to rein yourself in!

Do not make any new points in your conclusion and do not be tempted to repeat arguments, although emphasising key issues is normally appropriate. It is often sufficient to say: 'In conclusion, based on the arguments (or discussion or facts) provided above, I would advise Joe that . . .'. I can't emphasise enough that no tutor will ever ask you to merely 'tell all you know' on a particular topic, so don't think that taking this approach will suffice.

As well as planning your answers, do not forget to plan your time. Many undergraduate examinations are three hours in length; some have additional 'reading time'. Divide this time carefully between the number of questions that have to be answered and ensure that you do not spend too long on one answer to the detriment of the others. It is **very** important to ensure that you answer the requisite number of questions. If you are required, for example, to answer four questions, you are unlikely to obtain as many marks by answering three questions particularly well as you could by answering the required four reasonably well.

I hope that it is unnecessary to remind you to check the date, time and place of the examination! Do, however, ensure that you are aware of what you may take into the examination room with you. For example, it is often possible to take in an unannotated copy of EU legislation – which you should find invaluable *if* you have referred to it diligently throughout your course.

All that remains now is to wish you every success! (Yes, your tutors *do* want you to do well!!)

Index

absolute majority voting 63

accountability 50–2

acte clair 93–4

administrative acts liability 110

animal life protection 133

annulment actions 107–9
  basic issues 107–8
  grounds 111
  illegality plea 108–9
  outcome 111
  persons eligible 111
  preliminary references 108
  time limits 111

Austria 18

Belgium 8, 76

Cassis principles,
  first 125–6
  second 131

charges having equivalent
  basic principles 117
  effect 117–19
  for an inspection 119
  exceptions to rule 118
  interpretation/application 118
  for services provided 119
  treaty provision 117–18

citizenship
  see EU citizenship

co-decision 33–4

Commission
  see European Commission

Committee of Permanent
  Representatives (COREPER) 37

Committee of Regions 47

common customs tariff 116–17

competences 29

conferral 27

constitution, draft 18–19

consultation 33

contractual liability 109

COREPER (Committee of
  Permanent Representatives) 37

Council of Europe 7–8

Council of Ministers 37–40
  basic summary 39, 40
  co-ordination/supervision
    roles 39
  compositions and functions 37–8
  COREPER .37
  decision making 38–9
  legislative role 38, 62

Court of Auditors (CoA) 14, 46–7

Court of First Instance
  (CFI) 11, 17
  see also General Court

Court of Justice 43–6
  activism .44–5
  Advocate Generals 44
  basic summary 43, 46
  case law, importance 64
  functions and jurisdiction 44
  interpretive methods 44–5
  judges 43–4
  non-compliance 99

preliminary references/
   rulings 94–5
procedure .45
   see also General Court
Croatia 18
customs duties 116–22
   basic provisions 116–17
   equivalent effect *see* charges
   having equivalent effect
customs union 116–17
Cyprus 18
Czech Republic 18

damages actions 109–12
   administrative acts liability 111
   causal links 111–12
   conditions for liability 110–12
   contractual liability 109
   legislative acts liability 110
   locus standi 109–10
   non-contractual liability 109
   rights conferred on
     individuals 110
   seriousness of breach 110–11
   time-limit 109–10
decisions .58–9
   direct effect 77, 85
democracy .50–2
direct effect doctrine,
   application .85
   basic issues 71
   conditions 76–7
   creation .75–6
   and directives *see* directives
   original position 71–2
   principle 75
   sources application 77–9
directives,
   actions against private parties 84
   basic meaning 58
   definition of state 79–80
   and direct effect 78–9, 80, 85
   interpretive obligation 80
   as source of right/obligation 82

state liability for damages *see*
   Francovich principle
directorates-general (DGs) 41
discrimination,
   equality principle 66, 164–5
   service providers' protection 168
   see also indirect discrimination;
     non-discrimination principle;
     reverse discrimination
discriminatory internal
   taxation 120–1
   basic principles 120
   Court of Justice
     interpretation 120–1
   genuine internal taxation 120
   indirect 121
draft constitution 18–19

Economic and Social Committee
   (ESC) 47
economically active citizens 142
Eden, Sir Anthony 8
educational establishments,
   employment restrictions 157
employment tribunal 88
employment/workers' rights,
   basic rights 144
   Court of Justice approach to
     equal treatment 146–7
   Discrimination *see* indirect
     discrimination
   economically active persons 142
   equal treatment 145–6
   establishment *see* freedom of
     establishment
   exit/entry *see* exit/entry,
     employment rights
   job seekers 144
   limitation of rights 154, 161
   living in one state, working
     in another 149
   meaning of worker 143–4, 161
   procedural safeguards for
     expulsion 154–5

public health limitation 156, 157
public policy/security
  restrictions 153
public service restrictions 156–7
qualifications, recognition 165
remaining after employment
  has ceased 149
residence *see* residence,
  employment rights
to free movement 161
  see also workers' families, rights

enforcement
against member states 97–100
basic principles 87, 90,
                                  112–13
effectiveness of procedures 100–1
EU institutions *see* EU institutions,
  enforcement against
national courts *see* national courts
referrals *see* preliminary
  references/rulings
summary .113

equality principle 66

establishment
see freedom of establishment

Estonia 18

EU citizenship 140–2
economically active citizens 14
equal treatment with
  nationals 160–2
family members of EU
  citizen .141
importance 140–1
non-economically active
  citizens 158–60, 161
persons eligible 141
right of free
  movement 141–2, 161

EU institutions, enforcement
against .101–12
annulment *see* annulment
  actions
basic systems 101
failure *see* failure to act
judicial review *see* judicial review

European Atomic Energy
  Community (EURATOM) 9, 10
European Central Bank (ECB),
basic summary 46
creation 14
European Coal and Steel
  Community (ECSC) 8–9
European Commission 17, 40–3
actions brought by 97–9
administrative and executive
  role 42
basic summary 43
composition 40
functions 41
investigative powers 98
legislative role 41, 62
non-compliance 99
referral to Court of Justice 98–9
supervision by EP 35
supervisory functions 42
European Communities 10
European Council 11
composition and functions 36–7
supervision by EP 35
European Court of Justice (ECJ) . . 11, 43
  see also Court of Justice
European Economic Community
  (EEC) 9–10
Merger Treaty 1965 10–11
Single European Act 1986 11–13
UK admission 18
  see also European Union
European Investment Bank 47–8
European Law,
approach 1–2, 6
EU/national law,
  interaction 71, 84–6
importance .1
recognised legal databases 3
resources 3
study advice 2
study direction 5–6
terminology *see* terminology
  see also individual entries

European Monetary Union (EMU) . . .13
European Parliament
    (EP) 11, 14, 16, 17, 32–6
    basic summary 36
    budgetary role 34
    composition and functions 32
    legislative role 33–4, 62
    supervisory role 34
European Union (EU),
    dates and events 24–5
    draft constitution 18–19
    enlargement 18
    European Communities 10
    functions of government 27, 32
    future challenges 23
    influences on 51
    legal personality 68
    and member states 28–9
    origins .7–10
    'support, co-ordinate or
        supplement' role 29
    three pillared structure 14–15
    Treaty of Amsterdam 15–17
    Treaty of Nice 17
    see also European Economic
        Community; individual entries;
        Treaty on European Union;
        Treaty of Lisbon
Examinations,
    revision 171–2
    technique 172–4
exclusive competence 29
exit/entry rights,
    Court of Justice approach to
        employment restrictions 155–6
    employment rights 145
    freedom of establishment 164
    non-economically active
        citizens .159
    service providers 167–8
    workers' families 151

failure to act 106–7
    consequences of successful
        challenge 107

persons able to challenge 107
persons challengeable 106–7
procedure .107
federalism .27–8
Finland 18
first Cassis principle 125–6
four freedoms 115
France 8
Francovich principle,
    actions against private parties 84
    basic principle 82–3, 85
    development 83
    intentionality/voluntariness 84
    'sufficiently serious' breach 83–4
    as uniform EU remedy 90
free movement of goods,
    basic principles 115–16
    non-pecuniary barriers
        see non-pecuniary barriers
        to trade
    pecuniary barriers 116–22
    summary 129, 137
free movement of persons 139–40
freedom of establishment,
    basic provisions 162, 169
    definition of establishment 163
    discrimination see
        discrimination
    employed/self-employment,
        distinction 163
    enforcement of rights 166
    limitations 165–6
    natural/artificial legal
        persons .163–4
    official authority 166
    public health limitation 166
    public policy limitation 166
    public security limitation 166
    qualifications, recognition 165
    right 162–3
    and self employment 142
fundamental rights 66–8

De Gaulle, General 18

General Court (GC) 17, 45
  see also Court of Justice
general principles,
  basic summary 65
  equality 66
  function and status 65–6
  fundamental rights 66–8
Germany 8, 73, 75
Goods,
  definition 115–16
    see also free movement of
      goods
Greece 18

health protection 133
human life protection 133
Hungary 18

illegality plea 108–9
imports
  see measures having equivalent
    effect; quantitative restrictions
    on imports
indirect discrimination,
  access to employment
    market 147–8
  basic issues 147
  justification 148
indirect effect,
  background 80
  definition .85
  development 80–1
  incidental 81–2, 85
industrial property protection . . .134–5
inspection charges 119
institutional balance 49–50
institutional structure 31–2, 48
intergovernmentalism 28
internal market 11–12
internal taxation
  see discriminatory internal
    taxation

international agreements,
  direct effect 78
  empowerment 68
Italy 8, 82, 99

job seekers' rights 144
judicial review,
  acts challengeable 102
  applicants 103–5
  basic provision 102
  direct concern 105
  grounds for challenge 103
  individual concern
    requirement 104–5
  non-privileged applicants 103–4
  persons challengeable 102
  privileged applicants 103
  purpose 111
  regulatory acts 105–6
  time limits 106
juridicial activism 44–5

Laeken Declaration 19
Latvia 18
legal databases, recognised 3
legal personality 68
legislation
  see secondary legislation;
    treaties
legitimacy .50–2
life protection 133
Lithuania 18
Luxembourg,
  Compromise 39
  membership 8

Maastrict Treaty
  see Treaty on European Union
Macedonia 18
majority voting 63
Malta 18
Marshall Plan .7

measures having equivalent effect,
  basic issues 122
  Dassonville formula 124–5
  definition of measures 123
  discrimination 'in law and
    in fact' 127
  distinctly/indistinctly applicable
    measures 124
  dual burden on importers 127–8
  export restrictions 129–30
  impedance of market access 128
  judicial development 124
  meaning .124–5
  rule of reason 125–6
  selling arrangements/product
    requirements, distinction . . .126–7
  use restrictions 128–9

member states,
  actions brought by 99–100
  direct effect *see under* directives
  division of competences 28–9
  enforcement against 97
  liability for damages 82–4
  liability for damages *see*
    Francovich principle
  wide definitions 79–80, 115
    see also state liability for
      damages

Merger Treaty 1965 10–11

Monnet, Jean .8

mutual recognition 131, 136

national courts 87–8
  action availability 89
  basic principle 87–8, 90
  choice of court 88
  non-discrimination
    principle 82, 88
  procedures 88–9

national treasures, protection 134

nationality, discrimination 66

Netherlands 8, 75–6

non-contractual liability 109
  basic issues 122

non-discrimination principle 82, 88
  see also discrimination

non-economically active
  citizens 158–60, 161

non-pecuniary barriers to trade   122–36
  arbitrary discrimination 135
  barriers *see* measures having
    equivalent effect; quantitative
    restrictions on imports
  Court of Justice position on
    derogation 131
  derogation from prohibitions . .130–6
  disguised restriction on trade 135
  grounds for derogation 132–5
  harmonisation and derogation . . .132
  mutual recognition 131, 136
  proportionality 136
  provisions for derogation 130

North Atlantic Treaty
  Organization (NATO) 7

official authority derogation,
  freedom of establishment 166
  service providers 168

opinions 59

ordinary procedure 34

Organisation for Economic
  Co-operation 7

pecuniary barriers to trade 116–22
  enforcement of rules 121–2

persons, free movement 139–40

pillared structure: creation 14–15
  Treaty of Amsterdam 16–17

plant life protection 133

plea of illegality 108–9

Poland 18

Portugal 18

power sharing 27–31, 52–3

preliminary references/rulings,
  abstract/concrete theory 93
  acte clair .93–4

basic provisions 91
consequences 95–7
decision to refer 92–4
effects 91–2
obligation to refer 93
procedure 95, 96
purpose 91
referrals from national bodies 92
refusal by Court of Justice 94–5
primary sources
see treaties
proportionality 29–30, 136
public health,
employment limitation 156, 157
freedom of establishment
limitation 166
service provider derogation 168
public morality 132
public policy,
employment limitation 153
freedom of establishment
limitation 166
service provider derogation 168
trade restrictions 132–3
public security,
employment limitation 153
freedom of establishment
limitation 166
service provider derogation 168
trade restrictions 133

qualifications, recognition 165
qualified majority voting
(QMV) 38–9, 64
quantitative restrictions on
imports,
basic provisions 122–3
definitions 123–4
export restrictions 129–30

recommendations 59
regulations 58
direct effect 77, 85
regulatory acts 105–6

remedies,
availability .89
principles 89–90
uniform EU .90
residence rights,
Court of Justice approach to
employment restrictions 155–6
employment rights 145
freedom of establishment 164
non-economically active
citizens 159–60
workers' families 151
reverse discrimination 164–5
revision for examinations 171–2
rule of reason 125–6

Schuman, Robert 8
second Cassis principle 131
secondary legislation 57–62
actors in enactment 60
assent procedure 62
basic principles 57
categories .58–9
consultation procedure 62
enactment 59–62, 63
legal basis for creation 60
legislative procedures 60–1
ordinary legislative procedures . . .61
special legislative procedures 62
voting procedures 38–9, 63–4
self-employment, freedom of
establishment 142, 169
service charges 119
service providers,
basic rights 142, 167–8, 169
definition of service 167
discrimination protection 168
enforcement of rights 169
exceptions to right of free
movement 168, 169
and free movement 166–7, 169
official policy see official
policy derogation
shared competence 29

single market 11–12
Slovakia 18
Slovenia 18
social advantages 153
soft law 59
source of right/obligation, as
    directives 82
sources of law 55
Spaak, Paul-Henri 9
Spain...........................18
state liability for damages
    see Francovich principle
subsidiarity 29–30
supranationalism 28
supremacy doctrine,
    basic principle.................72
    creation 72
    development 73–5
Sweden........................18

taxation, internal
    see discriminatory internal
        taxation
terminology 3–5
    case names 4–5
    EEC/EC/EU, distinction 4
    jargon 3–4
        see also abbreviations;
            glossary
three pillared structure 14–15
treaties,
    creation 57
    direct effect 77, 85
    extant 56

ordinary/simplified revision
    procedures 57
Treaty of Amsterdam 1997 15–17
Treaty on European
    Union 1992 (Maastricht
    Treaty) 13–15
    changes to EEC Treaty 13–14
Treaty on European Union
    (Maastricht Treaty), three
    pillared structure 14–15
Treaty of Lisbon 16, 19
    changes 20–3
Treaty of Nice 17
Turkey 18

unanimity 64

Verheugen, Gunther 18
vertical direct effect 79–80
voting procedures 38–9, 63–4

workers' families, rights 149–53
    basic provisions 149–50
    basic rights 150–1, 161
    composition of family 150
    education rights 152
    exit/entry *see* exit/entry,
        employment rights
    general rights 153
    remaining after death/
        divorce 152–3
    residence *see* residence,
        employment rights
    social advantages 153
    taking up employment 151
        see also employment/workers' rights